Battle Orders • 37

The Roman Army of the Principate 27 BC–AD 117

Nic Fields

Consultant Editor Dr Duncan Anderson • *Series editors* Marcus Cowper and Nikolai Bogdanovic

First oublished in Great Britain in 2009 by Osprey Publishing Ltd.
Midland House, West Way, Botley, Oxford OX2 0PH, UK
443 Park Avenue South, New York, NY 10016, USA
E-mail: info@ospreypublishing.com

© 2009 Osprey Publishing Ltd.

A CIP catalogue record for this book is available from the British Library

Print ISBN: 978 1 84176 386 5
PDF e-book ISBN: 978 1 84603 868 6

Editorial by Ilios Publishing, Oxford, UK (www.iliospublishing.com)
Page layout, maps and diagrams by Bounford.com, Cambridge, UK
Typeset in Monotype Gill Sans and ITC Stone Serif
Index by Sandra Shotter
Originated by United Graphics Pte
Printed and bound in China through Bookbuilders

09 10 11 12 13   10 9 8 7 6 5 4 3 2 1

FOR A CATALOGUE OF ALL BOOKS PUBLISHED BY OSPREY MILITARY AND
AVIATION PLEASE CONTACT:

NORTH AMERICA
Osprey Direct, c/o Random House Distribution Center,
400 Hahn Road, Westminster, MD 21157
E-mail: uscustomerservice@ospreypublishing.com

ALL OTHER REGIONS
Osprey Direct, The Book Service Ltd, Distribution Centre,
Colchester Road, Frating Green, Colchester, Essex, CO7 7DW, UK
E-mail: customerservice@ospreypublishing.com

Key to first names (*praenomeninis*)

A.	Aulus	M'.	Manius
Ap.	Appius	P.	Publius
C.	Caius	Q.	Quintus
Cn.	Cnaeus	Ser.	Servius
D.	Decimus	Sex.	Sextus
L.	Lucius	Sp.	Spurius
M.	Marcus	T.	Titus
Mam.	Mamius	Ti.	Tiberius

Abbreviations

AE	*L'Année Épigraphique* (Paris, 1888–)
Campbell	B. Campbell, *The Roman Army, 31 BC–AD 337: A Sourcebook* (London, 1994)
CIL	T. Mommsen et al., *Corpus Inscriptionum Latinarum* (Berlin, 1862–)
Fink	R. O. Fink, *Roman Military Records on Papyrus* (New Haven, 1971)
ILS	H. Dessau, *Inscriptiones Latinae Selectae* (Berlin, 1892–1916)
P. Mich.	C.C. Edgar et al., *Papyri in the University of Michigan Collection* (Ann Arbor, 1931–)
RIB	R. S. O. Tomlin, *Roman Inscriptions of Britain 2* (Stroud, 1995)
Tab. Vindol. II	A. K. Bowman & J. D. Thomas, *The Vindolanda Writing-Tablets II* (London, 1994)

The Woodland Trust

Osprey Publishing are supporting the Woodland Trust, the UK's
leading woodland conservation charity, by funding the dedication
of trees.

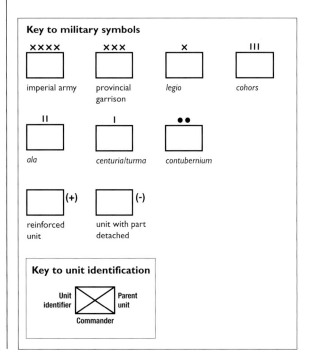

Contents

Introduction

Marble statue of Augustus as *imperator*, from 'Villa Livia' at Prima Porta (Vatican City, Musei Vaticani, inv. 2290). The decoration of the cuirass features the symbolic return of an *aquila* captured by the Parthians at Carrhae (53 BC). No soldier himself, Augustus was the commander-in-chief of a 'new model' army of his own making. (Fields-Carré Collection)

The professionalization of the Roman Army after Marius' reforms led directly to the use and abuse of consular power by individual generals seeking to usurp the power of the Senate. Consequently the last five decades of the Republic were characterized by two important features: the jostling for power and status by a number of dynamic political players, and the calamitous civil wars generated by their personal, be it selfish or altruistic, ambitions. It was the last of these republican warlords who was to emerge victorious as the first Roman emperor under the new name of Augustus. Officially he was addressed as *princeps* (e.g. *Res Gestae Divi Augusti* 13, 30.1, 32.3), that is the first citizen of the state, and his reign was the beginning of the Principate.

The army of the Principate established by Augustus drew heavily on the nomenclature and traditions of the dead Republic. But it was new. He decided to meet all the military needs of the empire from a standing, professional army, so that there was no general need to raise any levies through conscription (*dilectus*), which in actual fact he did on only two occasions, namely following the crises in Pannonia (AD 6) and Germania (AD 9). Military service was now a lifetime's occupation and career, and pay and service conditions were established that took account of the categories of soldier in the army: the praetorians (*cohortes praetoriae*), the citizen soldiers of the legions (*legiones*) and the non-citizens of the auxiliaries (*auxilia*). Enlistment was not for the duration of a particular conflict, but for 25 years (16 in the praetorians), and men were sometimes retained even longer (e.g. Tacitus *Annales* 1.17.3). At the end of service there was a fixed reward, on the implementation of which the soldier could rely. The loyalty of the new army was to the emperor, as commander-in-chief, and neither to the Senate nor the Roman people.

Cassius Dio, writing of the events of 29 BC, reports two speeches made before Augustus by his counsellors, M. Vipsanius Agrippa and C. Maecenas, in which the best way of securing the continuation of the Roman state and defence of its empire was discussed. Agrippa apparently advocated the retention of the traditional system (by which men would be conscripted to serve short periods, and then released into civilian life). Maecenas, on the other hand, argued for 'a standing army [*stratiôtas athanatous* in Cassius Dio's Greek] to be recruited from the citizen body [i.e. *legiones*], the allies [i.e. *auxilia*] and the subject nations' (52.27.1), and despite Agrippa's contention that such an army could form a threat to the security of the empire, carried the day.

Dialogues were a convention of ancient historiography, and these speeches need not be judged the true record of a real debate between the two. In part at least they reflect the political situation of Cassius Dio's own time and were aimed at a contemporary emperor, perhaps Caracalla (r. AD

211–17). Nevertheless in 13 BC, after he had returned from Gaul, Augustus ordained that terms of service in the legions should in future be fixed at 16 years, to be followed by a four-year period 'under the flag' (*sue vexillo*, hence *vexillarii*, a corps of veterans, a reserve), to be rewarded by a fixed cash gratuity, though this could be commuted to a plot of land, measuring 200 *iugera* (*c*.50 ha), in a veteran-colony in the provinces. In AD 5 some alterations were made to the conditions of service. The number of years that the new recruit had to serve under arms was upped to 20 years, with a further period (not specified, but probably at least five years) in reserve. The cash gratuity was now fixed at 3,000 *denarii* for an ordinary ranker, a lump sum the equivalent of over 13 years' pay (Cassius Dio 54.25.6, 55.23.1).

Seemingly as part of this same package, but recorded by Cassius Dio (55.25.2, cf. Suetonius *Divus Augustus* 49.2, Tacitus *Annales* 1.78.2) under the following year (AD 6), Augustus masterminded the creation of a military treasury (*aerarium militare*). Its function was to arrange the payment of bounties to soldiers. Augustus opened the account with a large gift of money from his own funds, some 170 million *sestertii* according to his own testimony (*Res Gestae Divi Augusti* 17.2), but in the longer term the treasury's revenues were to come from two new taxes imposed from this time onwards on Roman citizens: a five per cent tax on inheritances and a one per cent tax on auction sales in Rome. The introduction of these taxes caused uproar, but taxation was preferable to the displacement, acrimony and ruin which had been the consequences of land settlement programmes of the civil war years. Augustus thus shifted a part of the cost of the empire's defence from his own purse to the citizenry at large. But the wages of serving soldiers (225 *denarii* per annum for an ordinary ranker) continued to be paid by the imperial purse; Augustus could brook no interference, or divided loyalties there. The management of the army, particularly its pay and benefits, was from the start one of what Tacitus calls 'the secrets of ruling' (*Annales* 1.6). Power was protected and preserved by two things, soldiers and money. And so the security and survival of the emperor and his empire were now the sole responsibility of the emperor and his soldiers.

Altar (*RIB* 2092) dedicated to *Disciplina Augusti* by soldiers of cohors II Tungrorum *milliaria equitata* stationed at Birrens-Blatobulgium (Edinburgh, National Museums of Scotland). The cult links two concepts, namely, obedience to the emperor and military efficiency. The top of the altar is hollowed out to form a focus where offerings of fruit or grain may be deposited. (Fields-Carré Collection)

Roman military organization

A great body of information on the unit size and organization of the Roman Army has been amassed by the patient work of several generations of scholars. The literary sources are often obscure or contradictory on the details of unit structures, but much information has been derived from epigraphic and papyrological record as well as that of archaeology. As a result a fairly coherent picture of the army's structure has emerged.

Legion

Unsurprisingly, the army seems to have been most attractive as a definite career to the poorest citizens. For such men, the legions offered a roof over their head, food in their bellies and a regular income in coin. Basic military pay was not the road to riches, but there was always the chance of bounties and other cash gifts,

Relief showing four legionaries (Saintes, musée archéologique, E 1344 MAS-PB). The individual legions (and units of the *auxilia*) remained permanently in commission with the same numerals and titles, and were renewed by constant supplementation. The soldier served for an extended period, and looked on the army as a career. A proper financial structure ensured the payment of wages. (Fields-Carré Collection)

and the certainty of a discharge bonus. Overall a soldier's life was more secure than that of an itinerant labourer, and he enjoyed a superior status too. Of course we must remember the harsher side of such a career. A soldier ran the risk of being killed or crippled by battle or disease, but also on an everyday basis was subject to the army's brutal discipline. Yet to many people in the empire who lived at subsistence level, the well-fed soldier with his ordered existence in his well-built and clean camp must have seemed comfortably off. And so the legions became permanent units with their own numbers and titles and many were to remain in existence for centuries to come.

From Augustus onwards the emperor commanded 25 legions in total (28 before the Varian disaster of AD 9). Legions were probably in the order of 5,000 men strong (all ranks) and composed of Roman citizens. Legionaries were mostly volunteers, drawn initially from Italy (especially the north), but increasingly from the provinces. As the 1st century AD progressed, many recruits in the west were coming from the Iberian provinces, Gallia

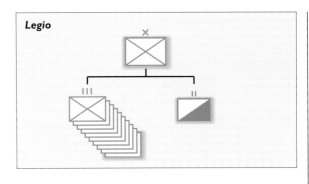

The main unit of the Roman Army, the *legio* was divided into ten *cohortes*, all of which, during the Iulio-Claudian era, were officially 480 strong. Attached to a *legio* was a body of mounted legionaries, known as the *equites legionis* and 120 strong.

Tombstone of Lucius Autius, son of Lucius, found at Camp d'Aulney, north of Saintes, dated post revolt AD 21 (Saintes, musée archéologique, 49.475). Born in Forum Iulii (Fréjus), Gallia Narbonensis, Autius was a *miles* of *legio XIIII Gemini*. He died age 35 having served for 15 years; he thus did not complete the statutory 25 years. (Fields-Carré Collection)

Legio

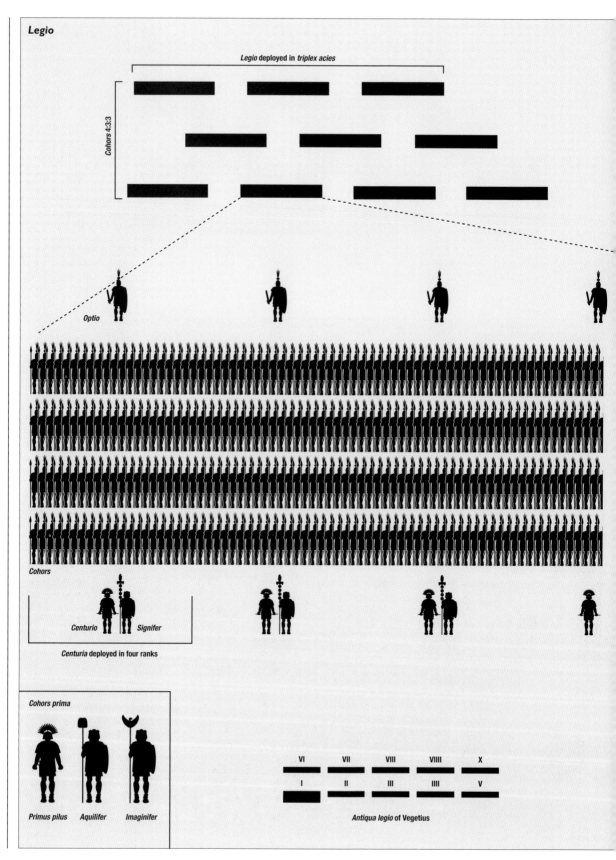

Legio deployed in *triplex acies*

Cohors 4:3:3

Optio

Cohors

Centurio   Signifer

Centuria deployed in four ranks

Cohors prima

Primus pilus   Aquilifer   Imaginifer

| VI | VII | VIII | VIIII | X |
| I | II | III | IIII | V |

Antiqua legio of Vegetius

Legion command

Legatus   Tribunus laticlavius   Praefectus castrorum   5 Tribuni angusticlavii

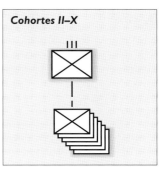

Cohortes II–X

The basic tactical unit of the Roman army, the regular *cohors* was subdivided into six *centuriae* of 80 men, each with a *centurio*.

When deployed for battle, the ten *cohortes* of a *legio* still formed up in the traditional *triplex acies*, with four in the front line, then a line of three, and finally three more at the rear, though a two-line battle formation might be adopted. The *antiqua legio* of Vegetius (2.4–14) probably reflects the *legio* of our period, and his description (2.6) of *cohortes* deployed for battle gives us some indication of their relative importance. In the front line the *cohors prima* was placed on the right, the position of honour, *cohors III* in the centre, *cohors V* on the left, while between them were *cohortes II* and *IIII*. In the second line on the right was *cohors VI*, which he says should consist of the finest of the young men. In the centre was *cohors VIII* with selected soldiers and *cohors X* on the left also with good soldiers, *cohortes VII* and *VIIII* coming between. It would be in this pair of *cohortes* that we would expect to find the newest recruits to the *legio*.

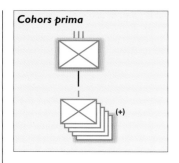

Cohors prima

At some date, probably at the beginning of the Flavian era, the *cohors prima*, the most senior, was increased in size from *quingenaria* to *milliaria*, and the number of *centuriones* in it reduced from six to five. Thus the *cohors prima* had only five *centuriae*, but of double the number of men. It seems logical to assume that the *cohors prima* included the legion's veterans.

The basic sub-unit of the Roman Army, a *centurio* was divided into ten *contubernia*, or 'tentfuls'. Each *contubernium* consisted of eight men who messed and slept together, sharing a tent on campaign and a pair of rooms in a barrack block. In the period from Augustus to Nero, a *legio* had 60 *centuriae*. This number was then reduced to 59, with five double-strength *centuriae* in the *prima cohors* and 54 standard *centuriae* in the other nine *cohortes*.

Narbonensis, and Noricum, and in the east from the Greek cities of Macedonia and Asia. Thus by the end of the century the number of Italians serving in the legions was small. Statistics based on nomenclature and the origins of individuals show that of all the legionaries serving in the period from Augustus to Caligula, some 65 per cent were Italians, while in the period from Claudius to Nero this figure was 48.7 per cent, dropping even further to 21.4 per cent in the period from Vespasianus to Traianus. Thereafter, the contribution of Italians to the manpower of the legions was negligible (Webster 1979: 108). It must be emphasized, however, that these statistics represent all legionaries in the empire. In reality, there was a dichotomy in recruitment patterns between the western and eastern provinces, with legions in the west drawing upon Gaul, Iberia and northern Italy, while those stationed in the east very quickly harnessed the local resources of manpower.

Part of Caesar's consular series formed in 48 BC, *III Gallica* had been serving in the east since Philippi (42 BC). The legion had fought well under Marcus Antonius against the Parthians (36 BC), as it was to do again under Cn. Domitius Corbulo (AD 57–63), and had been part of the garrison of Syria as early as 4 BC, if not before (Plutarch *Marcus Antonius* 42.11, Tacitus *Annales* 15.6, 25–26, Josephus *Bellum Iudaicum* 2.38). With the Flavian forces at Second Cremona, a battle fought through the hours of darkness, at dawn the soldiers of *III Gallica* turned in true eastern manner to salute the rising sun. The Vitellian army thought they were hailing reinforcements and fled (Tacitus *Historiae* 3.24.3–25.1, Cassius Dio 65.14.3). Recruiting locally (e.g. Tacitus *Annales* 13.7.1, 35.3), the legion had obviously acquired a tradition of worship of an oriental solar deity, perhaps Iuppiter Optimus Maximus Dolichenus, a warlike solar Baal directly associated with the creation of weapons with iron. After Cremona it was billeted for a time at Capua, and then stationed once more in Syria.

But this legion was not an anomaly. The men of Vitellius' Rhine legions, marching through northern Italy en route to Rome several months before Second Cremona, seemed to the local residents an uncouth and foreign band (Tacitus *Historiae* 2.21, cf. 4.65). An inscription (*ILS* 2304) from near Alexandria, dated AD 194, records the names of 46 soldiers who have just received their honourable discharge. Of the 41 whose origins are mentioned, 24 of these give the camp as their domicile, or more precisely 'born in the camp' (*origo castris*). It is likely that most of them were illegitimate sons born to soldiers from local women living in the nearby *canabae*, that is, the extramural settlement associated with the garrison.

Legions consisted of ten cohorts (*cohortes*), with six centuries (*centuriae*) of 80 men in each cohort, apart from the first cohort (*cohors prima*), which from AD 70 or thereabouts was double strength, that is five centuries of 160 men.

Centuria

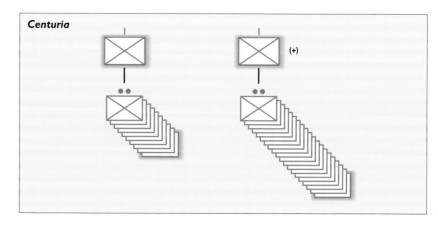

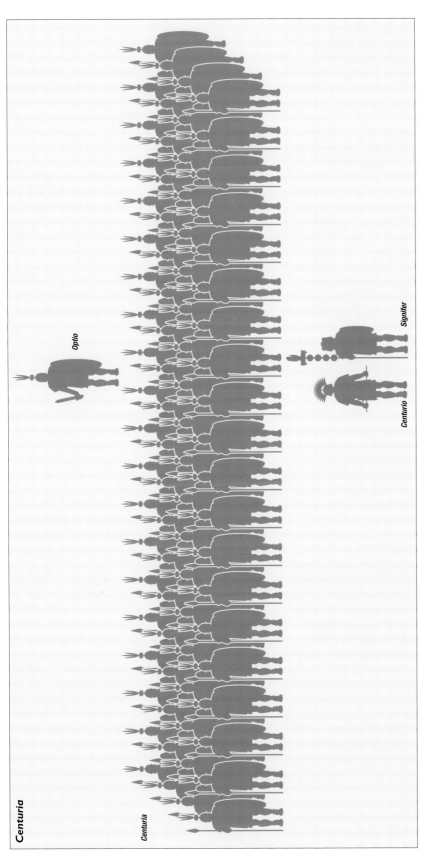

On the field of battle each *centuria* usually fought in four ranks, with one metre frontage for each file and two metres depth for each rank. This gave ample room for the use of *pilum* and *gladius*. The number of ranks could be doubled if extra solidity was required. In fact a convenient march formation was an eight-man wide column (i.e. one *contubernium*), and this only needed a right wheel, march to the flank, halt, front and double files to become a fighting formation. This graphic chart illustrates a *centuria legionis*.

Centuria

Optio

Signifer

Centurio

Centuria

Commanded by a centurion (*centurio*) and his second in command (*optio*), a standard-size century (*centuria*) was divided into ten eight-man sub-units (*contubernia*), each *contubernium* sharing a tent on campaign and pair of rooms in a barrack block, eating, sleeping and fighting together. Much like small units in today's regular armies, this state of affairs tended to foster a tight bond between 'messmates' (*contubernales*). Male bonding would explain why many soldiers (*milites*) preferred to serve their entire military career in the ranks despite the opportunities for secondment to specialized tasks and for promotion. Nonetheless, a soldier (*miles*) who performed a special function was excused fatigues, which made him an *immunis*, although he did not receive any extra pay (*Digesta* 50.6.7).

Finally there was a small force of 120 horsemen (*equites legionis*) recruited from among the legionaries themselves. These *equites* acted as messengers, escorts and scouts, and were allocated to specific centuries rather than belonging to a formation of their own. Thus the inscription (*RIB* 481) on a tombstone from Deva (Chester) describes an *eques* of *legio II Adiutrix pia fidelis* as belonging to the *centuria* of Petronius Fidus. Citizen cavalry had probably disappeared after Marius' reforms, and certainly was not in evidence in Caesar's legions. However, apart from a distinct reference to 120 cavalry of the legion in Josephus (*Bellum Iudaicum* 3.68), they seem not to have been revived as part of the Augustan reforms.

Detachments

When territory was added to the empire, a garrison had to be put together to serve in its defence. New legions were sometimes raised, but normally these green units were not themselves intended for service in the new province. So when an invasion and permanent occupation of Britannia became a hard possibility under Caligula, two new legions, *XV Primigenia* and *XXII Primigenia*, were formed in advance. Their intended role was as replacements for experienced legions earmarked to join the invasion force: *XV Primigenia* to release *legio XX* from Novaesium (Neuss), and *XXII Primigenia* to release *XIIII Gemina* from Mogontiacum (Mainz). The invasion force that eventually sailed for Britannia in the summer of AD 43 consisted of *XX* and *XIIII Gemina*, along with *II Augusta*, which had been at Argentoratum (Strasbourg), this camp was now left vacant, and *VIIII Hispana* from Siscia (Sisak) in Pannonia (Tacitus *Annales* 14.32.6).

Nevertheless, transfers of legions to different parts of the empire could leave long stretches of frontier virtually undefended, and wholesale transfers became unpopular as legions acquired local links. An extreme case must be that of *II Augusta*. Part of the invasion army of AD 43, this legion was to be stationed in the province for the whole time Britannia was part of the empire. As mentioned above, many recruits were the illegitimate sons of serving soldiers or veterans, that is to say, *origo castris*. Therefore, the custom developed of sending not an entire legion to deal with emergencies, but detachments drawn from the various legions of a province.

The erection of a temple to Mercury is recorded on this altar (*RIB* 2148) from Castlecary, Antonine Wall (Edinburgh, National Museums of Scotland). Dedicated by soldiers (*milites*) of *legio VI Victrix*, they give their *origines* as Italy and the province of Noricum. By the time this was erected in the mid-2nd century AD, the number of Italians joining the legions had fallen to below one per cent (Fields-Carré Collection)

Detachments from legions operating independently or with other detachments were known as *vexillationes*, named from the square flag, *vexillum*, which identified them. Until the creation of field armies in the late empire, these *vexillationes* were the method of providing temporary reinforcements to armies for major campaigns. Thus Domitius Corbulo received a *vexillatio* from *X Fretensis*, then stationed at the Euphrates crossing at Zeugma, during his operations in Armenia. Later he was to take three *vexillationes* of 1,000 men (i.e. two cohorts) from each of his three Syrian legions (*III Gallica*, *VI Ferrata* and *X Fretensis*) to the succour of Caesennius Paetus, whose army was retreating post-haste out of Armenia (Tacitus *Annales* 15.8–17).

This sculptural relief of three legionaries was found at Croy Hill, Antonine Wall (Edinburgh, National Museums of Scotland). It was probably the upper part of a tombstone showing a father, the deceased, flanked by his two sons. All three presumably served in *legio VI Victrix*, and illustrate the notion of recruits being drawn from those who gave their domicile as *origo castris*. (Fields-Carré Collection)

Auxiliaries

Under Augustus the rather heterogeneous collection of auxiliary units (*auxilia*) serving Rome was completely reorganized and given regular status within the new standing army. Trained to the same standards of discipline as the legions, the men were long-service professionals like the legionaries and served in units that were equally permanent. Recruited from a wide range of warlike peoples who lived just within or on the periphery of Roman control, with Gauls, Thracians and Germans in heavy preponderance, the *auxilia* were freeborn non-citizens (*peregrini*) who, at least from the time of Claudius, received full Roman citizenship on honourable discharge after completion of their 25 years under arms.

Tacitus tells us that the Batavi, on the lower Rhine, paid no taxes at all, but 'reserved for battle, they are like weapons and armour, only to be used in war'

Ala

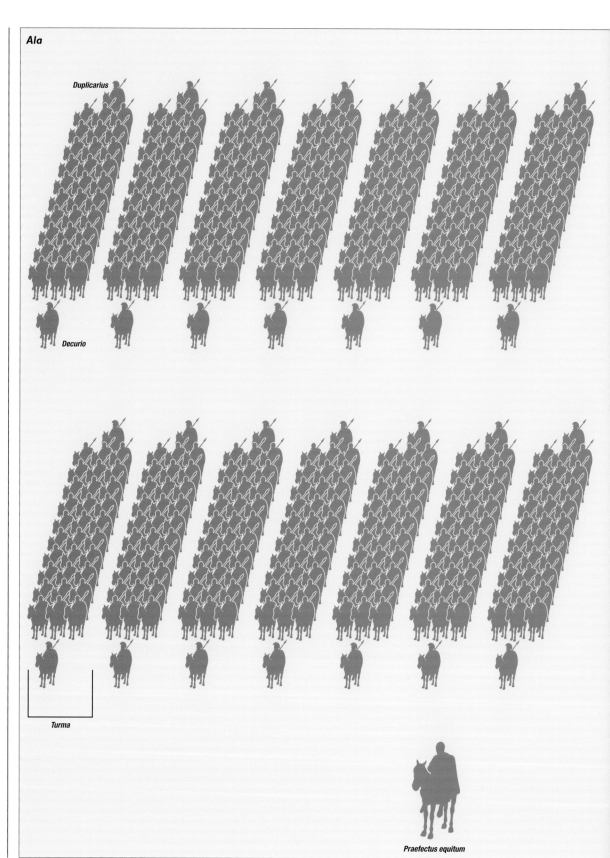

Duplicarius

Decurio

Turma

Praefectus equitum

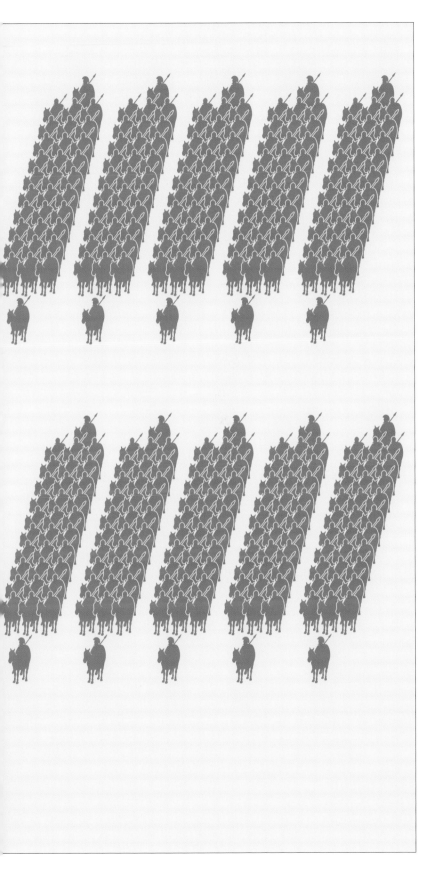

The *cohors peditata quingenaria* was clearly based on the legionary *cohortes II–X* as it consisted of six *centuriae* each 80 men strong though unlike a legionary cohort, a prefect (*praefectus cohortis*) commanded it. Under him, however, each *centuria* was led by a *centurio* who was assisted by an *optio*, *signifer* and *tesserarius*.

The *ala* was subdivided, not into *centuriae*, but into *turmae*. An *ala* would be either of 512 cavalrymen in 16 *turmae* (*quingenaria*), or of 768 cavalrymen in 24 *turmae* (*milliaria*). However, a prefect of cavalry (*praefectus equitum*, later *praefectus alae*) commanded both types. This graphic chart illustrates an *ala milliaria*.

Cohors peditata milliaria

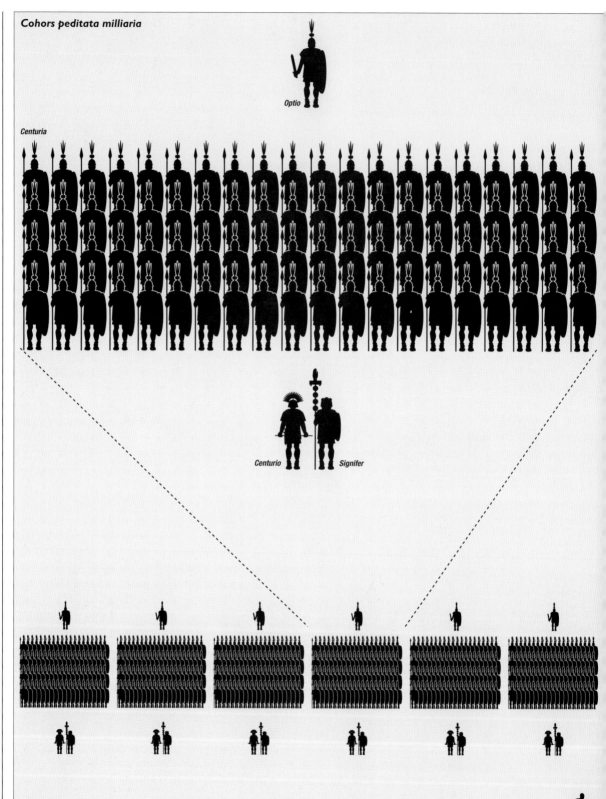

Optio

Centuria

Centurio   Signifer

Tribunus cohortis

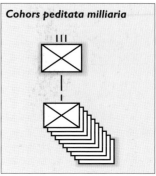

The *cohors peditata milliaria*, unlike the double-strength centuries of the *prima cohors* of a legion, was of ten *centuriae* each 80 men strong, a total of 800 men under the command of a tribune (*tribunus cohortis*). Again, each *centuria* was led by a *centurio* who was assisted by an *optio*, *signifer* and *tesserarius*.

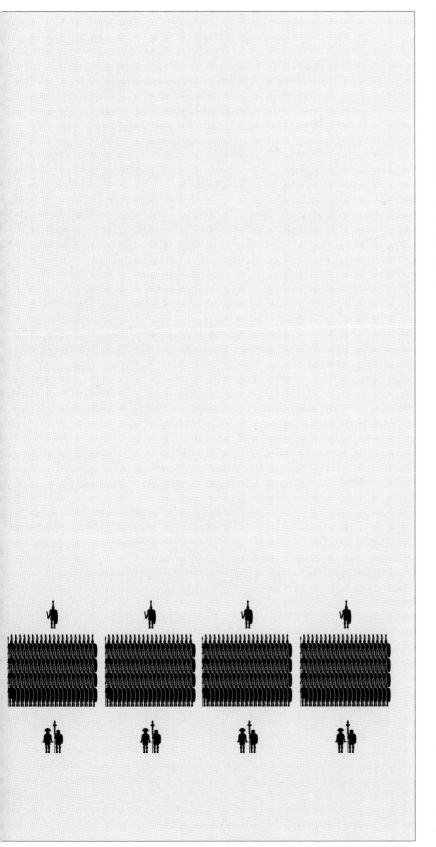

At full strength, the *cohors peditata* was either of 480 men (six centuries) or 800 men (ten centuries). The smaller *cohors* was called *quingenaria* (nominally 500) and the larger *milliaria* (nominally 1,000). This graphic chart illustrates a *cohors peditata milliaria*.

The *cohors equitata quingenaria* consisted of six *centuriae* and four *turmae*, a total of 480 infantrymen and 128 cavalrymen (6 x 80 + 4 x 32 = 608). A *cohors equitata quingenaria* was regularly commanded by a *praefectus cohortis*, who was an equestrian officer on the first step of the *tres militiae*.

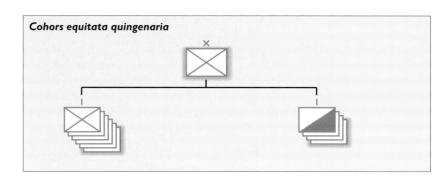

Cohors equitata quingenaria

The *cohors equitata milliaria* consisted of ten *centuriae* and eight *turmae*, a total of 800 infantrymen and 256 cavalrymen (10 x 80 + 8 x 32 = 1,056). A *cohors equitata milliaria* was regularly commanded by a *tribunus cohortis*, an equestrian officer on the second step of the *tres militiae*.

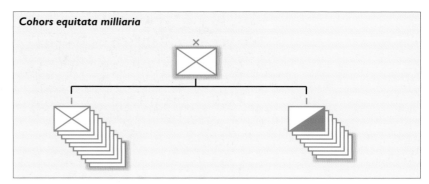

Cohors equitata milliaria

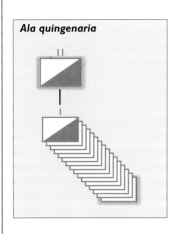

Ala quingenaria

The *ala quingenaria* consisted of 16 *turmae*, a total of 512 cavalrymen (16 x 32 = 512). Each *turma* was commanded by a *decurio*, the senior of whom was ranked as a *decurio princeps*.

(*Germania* 29). From him (*Historiae* 1.59, 2.27, 66, 4.12, *Annales* 2.8, 11) we hear of eight *cohortes* and one *ala*, nearly 5,000 warriors from the tiny region of Batavia, serving Rome at any one time. He also remarks of a *cohors Sugambrorum* under Tiberius, as 'savage as the enemy in its chanting and clashing of arms' (*Annales* 4.47.4) although fighting far from its Germanic homeland in Thrace. Further information concerning these tribal levies comes from Tacitus' account of the civil war. In AD 69, when Vitellius marched into Rome, his army also included 34 *cohortes* 'grouped according to nationality and type of equipment' (*Historiae* 2.89.2).

Take the members of *cohors II Tungrorum* for instance, who had been originally raised from among the Tungri who inhabited the north-western fringes of the Arduenna Silva (Ardennes Forest) in Gallia Belgica. Under the Iulio-Claudian emperors it was quite common for such units to be stationed in or near the province where they were first raised. However, the events of AD 68/69, with the mutiny of a large proportion of the *auxilia* serving on the Rhine, led to a change in this policy. Although the Roman high command did not abandon local recruiting, it did stop the practice of keeping units with so continuous an ethnic identity close to their homelands.

As expected, by the late 1st century AD, units were being kept up to strength by supplements from the province where they were now serving or areas adjacent to it. Such units retained their ethnic identities and names, even if they enlisted new recruits from where they were stationed. The epitaph of Sex. Valerius Genialis tells us that he was a trooper in *ala I Thracum*, and his three-part name that he was a Roman citizen. But it adds that he was a 'Frisian tribesman' (*RIB* 109). So, Genialis came from the lower Rhine, served in a Thracian cavalry unit stationed in Britannia and styled himself Roman.

Auxiliary cohorts were either 480 strong (*quingenaria*, 'five-hundred strong') or, from around AD 70, 800 strong (*milliaria*, 'one-thousand strong'). Known as *cohortes peditata*, these infantry units had six centuries with 80 soldiers to each if they were *quingenaria*, or if *milliaria* had ten centuries of 80 soldiers each. As in the legions, a centurion and an *optio* commanded a century, which was likewise divided into ten *contubernia*.

Low-cut relief decorating a column base from the *principia* of Mainz-Mogontiacum showing an auxiliary infantryman with oval *clipeus* and Coolus helmet (Mainz, Mittelrheinisches Landesmuseum). As well as a *lancea* in his right hand, he carries two spares in his left. Note the detail of his *caligae*. (Fields-Carré Collection)

The left-hand panel of the Bridgeness distance slab (No. 1), Antonine Wall (Edinburgh, National Museums of Scotland). The low-cut relief depicts a triumphant auxiliary trooper riding down four naked warriors. Equipped with what appears to be an oval *clipeus*, his *spatha* is carried in the unorthodox position on the right swinging from a wide baldric. (Fields-Carré Collection)

Cavalry units known as *alae* ('wings', it originally denoted the allies (*socii*) posted on the flanks) are thought to have consisted of 16 *turmae* (Hyginus 16, cf. *CIL* 3.6581), each with 30 troopers (Fink 80, cf. Arrian *Ars Tactica* 18.3) commanded by a *decurio* and his second-in-command the *duplicarius*, if they were *quingenaria* (512 total), or if *milliaria* 24 *turmae* (768 total). The latter units were rare; Britannia, for example, had only one in its garrison. Drawn from peoples nurtured in the saddle – Gauls, Germans, Iberians and Thracians were preferred – the horsemen of the *alae* provided a fighting arm in which the Romans were not so adept.

Additionally there were mixed foot/horse units, the *cohortes equitatae*. Their organization is less clear, but usually assumed, following Hyginus (26–27), to have six centuries of 80 men and four *turmae* of 30 troopers if *cohors equitata quingenaria* (608 total), or ten centuries of 80 men and eight *turmae* of 30 troopers

Cohors equitata quingenaria

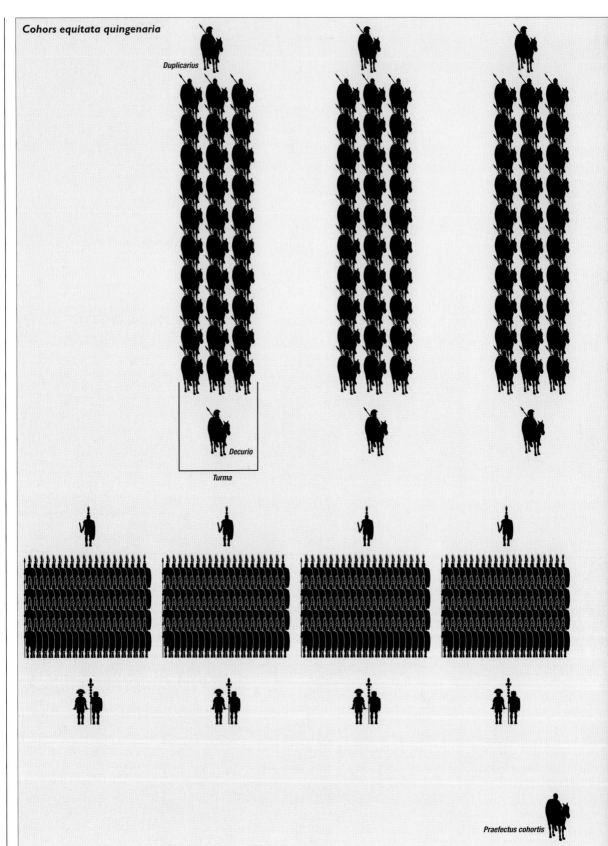

Duplicarius

Decurio

Turma

Praefectus cohortis

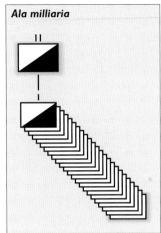

The *ala milliaria* consisted of 24 *turmae*, a total of 768 cavalrymen (24 x 32 = 768). Each *turma* was commanded by a *decurio*, the senior of whom was ranked as a *decurio princeps*.

Optio

Centurio   Signifer

Centuria

The *cohors equitata* was a mixed cohort based on the *centuria*, the infantry century commanded by a *centurio*, and the *turma*, the cavalry troop commanded by a *decurio*. Though these cavalrymen were not as well mounted as those serving in an *ala*, the *cohortes equitatae*, with their combination of foot and horse in a ratio of about four to one, were especially suited to garrison and local policing activities. This graphic chart illustrates a *cohors equitata quingenaria*, which consisted of six *centuriae* and four *turmae*.

The basic sub-unit of the Roman cavalry, at full strength the *turma* consisted of 32 men. This meant the *ala quingenaria* had 512 cavalrymen, and the *ala milliaria* 768 cavalrymen. Each *turma* was commanded by a *decurio* and his second-in-command a *duplicarius*.

Turma

Duplicarius

Decurio

if *cohors equitata milliaria* (1,056 total). An inscription, dated to the reign of Tiberius, mentions a *praefectus cohortis Ubiorum peditum et equitum*, 'prefect of a cohort of Ubii, foot and horse' (*ILS* 2690), which is probably the earliest example of this type of unit. It may be worth noting here that this Tiberian unit was recruited from the Ubii, a Germanic tribe distinguished for its loyalty to Rome (Tacitus *Germania* 28). In Gaul Caesar had employed Germanic horse-warriors who could fight in conjunction with foot-warriors, operating in pairs (Caesar *Bellum Gallicum* 7.65.5, 8.36.4, cf. Tacitus *Germania* 6).

Organized, disciplined and well trained, the pride of the Roman cavalry were obviously the horsemen of the *alae*, but more numerous were the horsemen of the *cohortes equitatae*. Having served for some time as infantrymen before being upgraded and trained as cavalrymen, these troopers were not as highly paid, or as well mounted as their brothers of the *alae*, but they performed much of the day-to-day patrolling, policing and escort duties.

Weapons and equipment

As with all professional, state-sponsored armies, improvements in equipment took place relatively slowly, necessitating the continued use of material that was of considerable age, even if certain older items, helmets in particular, were relegated to inferior grades of soldier. It may be said with truth of Roman arms that as long as a piece remained in serviceable condition, it continued to be used.

Helmets

Roman helmets, of Celtic inspiration, were made of iron or copper alloy (both bronze and brass are known). Bronze was a more expensive metal, but cheaper to work into a helmet: whereas iron helmets could only be beaten into shape, bronze ones were often 'spun' on a revolving former (a shaped piece of wood or stone) from annealed bronze sheet.

Whatever the material or type (e.g. Coolus, Imperial Gallic), however, the main features were the skull-shaped bowl, a large neck-guard to protect from blows to

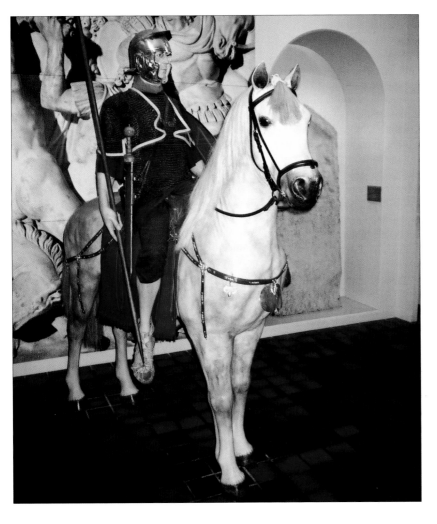

Full-size manikin of an auxiliary trooper (Cirencester, Corinium Museum). A characteristic feature of cavalry helmets is the extension of the cheek-pieces to cover the ears, commonly shaped as simulated ears. The model is also wearing a Gallic-type mail shirt with shoulder-cape. Note the *spatha* hangs at the right hip. (Fields-Carré Collection)

Bronze Coolus type 'E' helmet thought to have been found in the Thames (London, British Museum, P&E 1950 7-61). With its larger neck-guard and the addition of a brow-guard, the Coolus helmet started to replace the Montefortino pattern that had been commonly worn by legionaries of Caesar's legions. (Fields-Carré Collection)

the neck, cheek-pieces to protect the sides of the face – these were hinged so they could move freely – and a brow-guard, which defended against downward blows to the face. The helmet invariably left the face and ears exposed, since the soldier needed to see and hear to understand and follow battlefield commands. Soldiers often punched or scratched their names and those of their centurions onto their helmets to prevent mistaken ownership or indeed theft.

Unlike infantry helmets, cavalry helmets had extensions of their cheek-pieces to cover the ears. Often shaped as simulated ears, the extra protection to the face was clearly considered to be more important than some loss of hearing. Also the nape-guard was very deep, reaching down to close to the shoulders, but not wide, since this would have made the rider likely to break his neck if he fell from his horse. The cavalry helmet, therefore, protected equally well against blows to the side and the back of the head, vital in a cavalry mêlée when the two sides soon become intermingled.

Body armour

The Romans employed three main types of body armour: mail (*lorica hamata*), scale (*lorica squamata*) and segmented (*lorica segmentata*, a term coined during the Renaissance).

All body armour would have been worn over some kind of padded garment and not directly on top of the tunic. Apart from making the wearer more comfortable, this extra layer complemented the protective values of each type of armour, and helped to absorb the shock of any blow striking the armour. The anonymous author of the *De rebus bellicis*, an amateur military theoretician writing in the late 4th century AD, describes the virtues of such a garment: 'The ancients [i.e. the Romans], among the many things, which ... they devised for use in war, prescribed also the *thoracomachus* to counteract the weight and friction of armour. ... This type of garment is made of thick sheep's wool felt to the measure ... of the upper part of the human frame ...'. The author himself probably coined the term *thoracomachus* (cf. Greek *thorâx*, breastplate), which seems to be a padded garment of linen stuffed with wool. One illustration on Trajan's Column (Scene cxxviii) depicts two dismounted troopers on sentry duty outside a headquarters who appear to have removed their mail-shirts to expose the padded garment.

Lorica hamata

Mail was normally made of iron rings, on average about one millimetre thick and three to nine millimetres in external diameter. Each ring was connected to

Bronze scales from Newstead-Trimontium (Edinburgh, National Museums of Scotland). Each scale has four side-link holes and one lacing hole at the top. This piece dates to the end of the 1st century AD and probably belonged to a cavalryman stationed at the fort. The site itself has yielded no fewer than 346 scales to date. (Fields-Carré Collection)

four others, each one passing through the two rings directly above and two directly below – one riveted ring being inter-linked with four punched rings. The wearer's shoulders were reinforced with 'doubling', of which there were two types. One had comparatively narrow shoulder 'straps', and a second pattern, probably derived from earlier Celtic patterns, in a form of a shoulder-cape. The second type required no backing leather, being simply drawn around the wearer's shoulder girdle and fastened with S-shaped breast-hooks, which allowed the shoulder-cape to move more easily. The shoulder-cape is indicated on numerous grave markers belonging to cavalrymen, which also show the mail-shirt split at the hips to enable the rider to sit a horse.

Although mail had two very considerable drawbacks – it was extremely laborious to make, and while it afforded complete freedom of movement to the wearer, it was very heavy (10–15kg) – such armour was popular. A mail-shirt was flexible and essentially shapeless, fitting more closely to the wearer's body than other types of armour. In this respect it was comfortable, whilst the wearing of a belt helped to spread its considerable weight, which would otherwise be carried entirely by the shoulders. Mail offered reasonable protection, but could be penetrated by a strong thrust or an arrow fired at effective range.

Lorica squamata

Scale armour was made of small plates, one to five centimetres in length, of copper alloy, or occasionally of iron, wired to their neighbours horizontally and then sewn in overlapping rows to linen or leather backing. Each row was arranged to overlap the one below by a third to a half the height of the scales, enough to cover the vulnerable stitching. The scales themselves were thin, and the main strength of this protection came from the overlap of scale to scale, which helped to spread the force of a blow.

A serious deficiency lies in the fact that such defences could be quite readily pierced by an upward thrust of sword or spear, a hazardous aspect of which many cavalrymen must have been acutely aware when engaging infantry. This weakness was overcome, certainly by the 2nd century AD, when a new form of semi-rigid cuirass was introduced where each scale, of a relatively large dimension, was wired to its vertical, as well as its horizontal, neighbours.

Scale could be made by virtually anyone, requiring patience rather than craftsmanship, and was very simple to repair. Though scale was inferior to mail, being neither as strong nor as flexible, it was similarly used throughout our period and proved particularly popular with horsemen and officers as this type of armour, especially if tinned, could be polished to a high sheen. Apart from those to cavalry, most of the funerary monuments that depict scale armour belong to centurions.

Lorica segmentata

This was the famous laminated armour that features so prominently on the spiral relief of Trajan's Column. Concerning its origins, one theory suggests that it was inspired by gladiatorial armour, since these fighters are known to have worn a form of articulated protection for the limbs. Part of a *lorica segmentata* was found at the site of the Varian disaster, making this the earliest known example of this type of armour.

The armour consisted of some 40 overlapping, horizontal curved bands of iron articulated by internal straps. It was hinged at the back, and fastened with buckles, hooks and laces at the front. As the bands overlapped it allowed the wearer to bend his body, the bands sliding over one another. The armour was strengthened with back and front plates below the neck, and a pair of curved shoulder-pieces. In addition, the legionary would wear a metal studded apron hung from a wide leather belt (*cingulum*), which protected the belly and groin. Round the neck was worn a woollen scarf (*focale*), knotted in front, to prevent the metal plates from chafing the skin.

It was superior to mail with regard to ease of manufacture and preservation, but most particularly in view of its weight, this could be as little as 5.5kg, depending on the thickness of the plate used. It was also more resistant to much heavier blows than mail, preventing serious bruising and providing better protection against a sharp pointed weapon or an arrow. Its main weakness lay in the fact that it provided no protection to the wearer's arms and thighs. Also full-scale, working reconstructions of *lorica segmentata* have shown that the multiplicity of copper-alloy buckles, hinges and hooks, and leather straps, which gave freedom of movement, were surprisingly frail. It may have been effective against attacking blows or in impressing the enemy, but with its many maintenance problems we can understand why *lorica segmentata* never became standard equipment in the Roman Army.

Shields

Legionaries carried a large dished shield (*scutum*), which had been oval in the republican period but was now rectangular in shape. Besides making it less

Reconstruction of a 'cut-down'-style *scutum* in use by Augustus' time, exterior view (Caerleon, National Roman Legion Museum). The face was decorated with the unit's insignia – either in applied panels or painted. However, it is not clear whether the entire legion shared a common shield device, or whether each cohort was distinguished in some way, perhaps by colour. (Fields-Carré Collection)

burdensome, the shortening of the *scutum* at top and bottom was probably due to the introduction into the army of new combat techniques, such as the famous Roman 'tortoise' (*testudo*), a mobile formation entirely protected by a roof and walls of overlapping and interlocking *scuta* (e.g. Josephus *Bellum Iudaicum* 3.273). On the other hand, auxiliaries, infantrymen and horsemen alike, carried a flat shield (*clipeus*), with a variety of shapes (oval, hexagonal, rectangular) recorded.

Shields, *scuta* and *clipi* equally, were large to give their bearer good protection. To be light enough to be held continually in battle, however, shield-boards were usually constructed of double or triple thickness plywood made up of thin strips of birch or plane wood held together with glue. The middle layer was laid at right angles to the front and back layers. Covered both sides with canvas and rawhide, they were edged with copper-alloy binding and

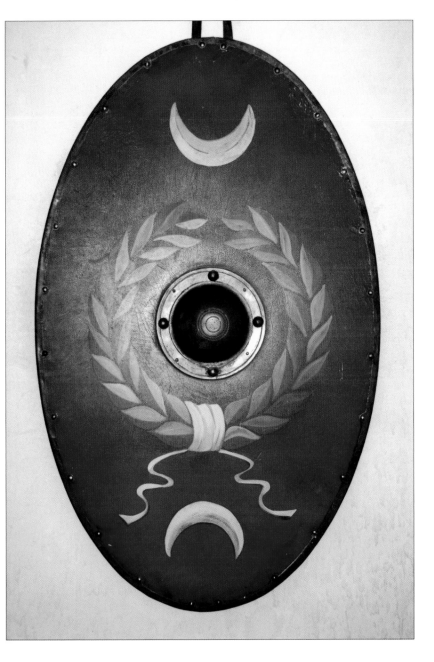

Reconstruction of an oval *clipeus*, the typical flat shield carried by auxiliary infantrymen and cavalrymen alike (Cirencester, Corinium Museum). An oval *clipeus* was only slightly lighter than a cylindrical *scutum*, its greater height compensating for the latter's greater width. (Fields-Carré Collection)

had a central iron or copper-alloy boss (*umbo*), a bowl-shaped protrusion covering a horizontal handgrip and wide enough to clear the fist of the bearer.

When not in use shields were protected from the elements by leather shield-covers; plywood can easily double in weight if soaked with rain. Oiled to keep it both pliant and water resistant, the cover was tightened round the rim of the shield by a drawstring. It was not unusual for it to have some form of decoration, usually pierced leather appliqué-work stitched on, identifying the bearer's unit. A cavalryman had the luxury of carrying his shield obliquely against the horse's flank (ibid. 3.96), slung from the two side horns of the saddle and sometimes under the saddlecloth (Trajan's Column scenes v, xlii, xlix, lxxxix, civ).

Shafted weapons

Pilum

Reconstruction of a *pilum* (Caerleon, National Roman Legion Museum). Instead of having the whole business end tempered, the tempering was confined to the pyramidal iron head. This ensured that the iron shank remained quite soft and liable to buckle and bend under the weight of the wooden shaft. (Fields-Carré Collection)

Since the mid-3rd century AD the *pilum* had been employed by legionaries in battle as a short-range shock weapon; it had a maximum range of 30m or thereabouts, although probably it was discharged within 15m of the enemy for maximum effect (Junkelmann 1991: 188). By our period the *pilum* had a pyramidal iron head on a long, untempered iron shank, some 60–90cm in length, fastened to a one-piece wooden shaft, which was generally of ash. The head was designed to puncture shield and armour, the long iron shank passing through the hole made by the head.

Once the weapon had struck home, or even if it missed and hit the ground, the soft iron shank tended to buckle and bend under the weight of the shaft. With its aerodynamic qualities destroyed, it could not be effectively thrown back, while if it lodged in a shield, it became extremely difficult to remove (Caesar *Bellum Gallicum* 1.25.3). Put simply, the *pilum* would either penetrate flesh or become useless to the enemy. Modern experiments have shown that a *pilum*, thrown from a distance of 5m, could pierce 30mm of pinewood or 20mm of plywood (Bishop & Coulston 1993: 48).

Continuing the practice of the late Republic, there were two fixing methods at the start of our period, the double-riveted tang and the simple socket reinforced by an iron collet. With regards to the tanged *pilum*, however, there is iconographical evidence, such as the Cancellaria relief and the Adamklissi monument, to suggest that a bulbous lead weight was now added under the pyramid-shaped wooden block fixing the shank to the shaft. Presumably this development was to enhance the penetrative capabilities of the *pilum* by concentrating even more power behind its small head, but, of course, the increase in weight would have meant a reduction in range.

Lancea

Auxiliary foot and horse used a light spear (*lancea*) as opposed to the *pilum*. Approximately 1.8m in length, it was capable of being thrown further than a *pilum*, though obviously with less effect against armoured targets, or retained in the hand to thrust over-arm as shown in the cavalry tombstones of the period.

Even though such funerary carvings usually depict troopers either carrying two *lanceae* or grooms (*calones*) behind them holding spares, Josephus claims (*Bellum Iudaicum* 3.96) Vespasianus' eastern cavalry carried a quiver containing three or more darts with heads as large as light spears. He does not say specifically where the quiver was positioned but presumably it was attached to the saddle. Arrian (*Ars Tactica* 40.10–11) confirms this in his description of an equestrian exercise in which horsemen were expected to throw as many as 15, or, in exceptional cases 20 light spears, in one run. Presumably infantrymen carried more than one *lancea*; a low-cut relief recovered from the site of the fortress at Mainz (Mogontiacum) depicts an auxiliary infantryman brandishing one in his right hand with two more held behind his *clipeus*. Analysis of the remains of wooden shafts shows that ash and hazel were commonly used.

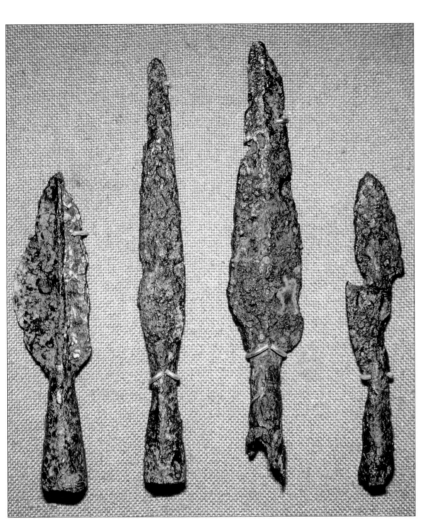

Selection of Roman iron spearheads from Roman Britain. These have tubular shanks and sockets to permit riveting to shafts. Carried by auxiliary infantrymen and cavalrymen alike, *lanceae* were fairly light, and could be thrown or kept in hand for close-quarter combat. (Ancient Art & Architecture)

Bladed weapons

Gladius

Back in the 3rd century BC the Romans had adopted a long-pointed, double-edged Iberian weapon, which they called the *gladius Hispaniensis* ('Iberian sword'), though the earliest specimens date to the turn of the 1st century BC. In our period the gladius was employed not only by legionaries, but by auxiliary infantrymen too.

Based on *gladii* found at Pompeii and on several sites along the Rhine and Danube frontiers, Ulbert (1969) has been able to show that there were two models of *gladius*, the one succeeding the other. First was the long-pointed 'Mainz' type, whose blade alone could measure 69cm in length and six centimetres in width (Connolly 1997: 49–56), and is well evidenced in the period from Augustus to Caligula. The 'Pompeii' type followed this, a short-pointed type that replaced it, probably during the early part of Claudius' reign. This pattern was shorter than its predecessor, being between 42 and 55cm long, with a straighter blade 4.2 to 5.5cm wide and short triangular point. Whereas the 'Mainz' type weighed between 1.2 and 1.6kg, the 'Pompeii' type was lighter, weighing about one kilogramme.

The blade of both types was a fine piece of steel with a sharp point and honed-down razor-sharp edges and was designed to puncture armour. It had a comfortable bone handgrip grooved to fit the fingers, and a large spherical pommel, usually of wood or ivory, to help with counter-balance.

Unusually, legionaries and auxiliaries carried their sword on the right-hand side suspended by the *cingulum* worn around the waist. The wearing of the sword on the right side goes back to the Iberians, and before them, to the Celts. The sword was the weapon of the high-status warrior, and to carry one was to display a symbol of rank and prestige. It was probably for cultural reasons alone, therefore, that the Celts carried their long slashing-sword on the right side. Customarily a sword was worn on the left, the side covered by the shield, which meant the weapon was hidden from view. However, the Roman soldier wore his sword on the right-hand side not for any cultural reason. As opposed

The 'Fulham' *gladius*, found in the Thames in that part of London. It is housed in its bronze decorated scabbard, which bears an embossed panel showing the she-wolf suckling Romulus and Remus. The 'Fulham' is an example of the long-pointed 'Mainz'-type *gladius*. (© The Trustees of the British Museum)

to a scabbard-slide, the four-ring suspension system on the scabbard enabled him to draw his weapon quickly with the right hand, an asset in close-quarter combat. By inverting the hand to grasp the hilt and pushing the pommel forwards he drew the *gladius* with ease.

Spatha

Cavalrymen, on the other hand, used a longer, narrower double-edged sword (*spatha*) that followed Celtic types, with a blade length from 64.5 to 91.5cm and width from four to six centimetres. The middle section of the blade was virtually parallel-edged, but tapered into a rounded point. It was intended primarily as a slashing weapon for use on horseback, though the point could also be used.

In spite of its length, the *spatha* was worn on the right side of the body, as Josephus says (*Bellum Iudaicum* 3.96) and numerous cavalry tombstones confirm, suspended from a waist belt or baldric whose length could be adjusted by a row of metal buttons. At the turn of the 2nd century AD, however, the *spatha* started to be worn on the left side, although not exclusively so.

Pugio

The *pugio* – a short, edged, stabbing weapon – was the ultimate weapon of last resort. However, it was probably more often employed in the day-to-day tasks of living on campaign. Carried on the left-hand side and suspended on the

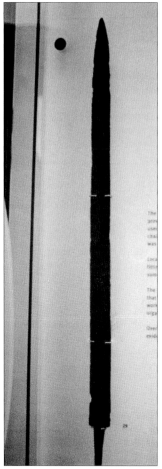

The blade of a *spatha* found at Newstead-Trimontium (Edinburgh, National Museums of Scotland). This example gives a good idea of the longer, slimmer swords used by cavalrymen. The organic hilt has perished thus leaving the tang from the blade exposed. (Fields-Carré Collection)

Buckle and decorative plaque from a *cingulum*, and three narrow plates and one terminal from an apron, all recovered from the battle site at Kalkriese (Bramsche, Museum und Park Kalkriese). The *cingulum* and apron became a proud mark of the soldier, who often paid good money for handsome decoration. Thus belt fittings were almost always tinned or silvered; these bronze examples are silvered. (akg-images/Museum Kalkriese)

First-century *pugio* from Pompeii with iron blade and bone hilt (Naples, Museo Archeologico Nazionale, inv. 5681). A *pugio* was regarded as a personal weapon and a tool, and its scabbard decoration subject to an individual's taste (and purse). It seems even ordinary rankers were quite prepared to invest considerable sums on decorated daggers and scabbards. (Fields-Carré Collection)

same *cingulum* that carried the sword (though two separate belts crossed 'cowboy' style was a dashing alternate), the *pugio* was slightly waisted in a leaf-shape and some 20 to 25.4cm long. The choice of a leaf-shaped blade resulted in a heavy weapon, to add momentum to the thrust. Like the *gladius*, the *pugio* was borrowed from the Iberians and then developed; it even had the four-ring suspension system on the scabbard, characteristic of the *gladius*.

The *pugio*, worn by legionaries and auxiliaries alike, was obviously a cherished object. The highly decorative nature of Roman daggers of our period, and particularly their sheaths, suggests that even common soldiers were prepared to spend considerable sums of money on what could be classified as true works of art. Though remaining an effective fighting weapon, the *pugio* was plainly an outward display of its wearer's power.

Command and control

Commanders had to maintain discipline among the soldiers under their command, keep order in their province and defend it against external attack. They had, therefore, to be men of education and status, for they must, in the name of the emperor, give commands and inspire respect. In the context of Roman society, even under the emperors, this meant that the commanders were invariably drawn from the aristocracy.

The Roman aristocracy, which made up a mere two per cent of the citizen population, was divided into two orders, the senatorial order (*ordo senatorius*) and the equestrian order (*ordo equester*). In fact most commanders of our period were senators, which is not surprising since traditionally the senatorial order commanded the armies of Rome and Augustus desired to provide them with opportunities to win fame and distinction in the traditional way. Indeed the senatorial order, with its long experience of government and military life, was initially the only body capable of providing enough men to govern the provinces and command the armies. However, these men were no longer the proconsuls or propraetors as of old, but representatives of the emperor himself. Likewise, as we shall soon discover, an increasing number of equestrians were being granted important commands.

Legion command

The legion's commanding officer was a legate (*legatus Augusti legionis*), appointed from the senatorial order by the emperor to command in his name, and by the

The right-hand panel of the Bridgeness distance slab (No. 1), Antonine Wall (Edinburgh, National Museums of Scotland). The low-cut relief depicts a purification ritual known as a *suovetaurilia*, with a bull, sheep and pig being led to sacrifice at an altar. The person officiating may be A. Claudius Charax from Pergamon (*AE* 1961.320), legate of *legio II Augusta c.* AD 143. (Fields-Carré Collection)

end of the Iulio-Claudian era only a senator who had already served as praetor was eligible. The command of a legion, therefore, now had a definite place in the hierarchy of the senatorial order, and was usually held for a period of about three years. At a later stage, after having held a consulship, a senator would have become a governor and, if in an armed province, ranked as a *legatus Augusti pro praetore* ('praetorian legate of Augustus') and have control over the legions stationed there. Thus the emperor governed through his *legati*, who held delegated power or *imperium*.

The other senior officers of a legion were six military tribunes, one of senatorial rank (*tribunus militum laticlavius*, 'with the broad purple strip on the toga'), the others equestrians (*tribuni militum angusticlavii*, 'with the narrow purple strip on the toga'), and 60 (later 59) centurions. In the hierarchy of command the senatorial tribune always ranked next to the legate, by virtue of his noble birth, and thus acted as the second-in-command of the legion. He served a short term as tribune before he was 25 years of age, prior to entering the Senate as a quaestor, a junior magistrate who administered financial matters in Rome or out in one of the provinces. He could look forward to receiving full command of a legion later in his senatorial career.

Next in order of seniority came not the remaining five tribunes, but the prefect of the camp (*praefectus castrorum*). A creation of Augustus, the post

M. Vipsanius Agrippa (64/63–12 BC)
Though of obscure origins, M. Vipsanius Agrippa, life-long friend and closest associate of Augustus, proved himself a man of considerable talent and energy. Augustus himself was no soldier, and it was even rumoured that he had fled the field during the first engagement at Philippi. It was Agrippa who was largely

responsible for the defeat of the combined forces of Marcus Antonius and Cleopatra at Actium, the battle that brought an end to five decades of civil unrest and political violence, and had followed this with a number of important military and diplomatic missions. He campaigned in Iberia, Gaul, on the Rhine and the Danube with great success, and in 23 BC was appointed to govern Syria and to oversee the eastern provinces (Cassius Dio 53.32.1, Josephus *Antiquitates Iudaicae* 15.350).

Agrippa was consul in 37 BC, 28 BC and 27 BC, and censor with Augustus in 28 BC. He was first married to Caecilia Attica, the heiress daughter of Cicero's close friend and confident Atticus, then to Marcella, the elder daughter of Augustus' sister Octavia, and finally, in 21 BC, to Iulia, the 18-year-old daughter of Augustus, presumably with the idea that while he might control affairs in the event of Augustus' death, power would at least eventually pass to one of the emperor's line. This third marriage was

certainly fruitful, producing five children in less than ten years, the two princes Caius and Lucius (Augustus adopting both in 17 BC), Iulia minor (who would match her mother's reputation for waywardness and likewise suffer permanent exile), Agrippina major (the mother of Caligula) and Agrippa Postumus (adopted by Augustus in AD 4, but banished three years later for violence and depravity, and liquidated immediately after Augustus' death). He deputized for Augustus when the emperor was in Iberia in 25 BC, was handed Augustus' signet ring when the emperor lay seriously ill in 23 BC, and was granted *imperium pro consule* later in the same year and sent east, which was renewed in 18 BC and made *maius* in 13 BC. In 18 BC *tribunicia potestas* was also granted to him for five years, and again for another five years in 13 BC. The following year, however, he died.

required considerable and detailed knowledge of the legion, its personnel and the daily rounds of duties. As the name implies, the *praefectus castrorum* had general charge of the camp, including the building and maintenance of it (Tacitus *Annales* 12.38.3, 13.39.2). In addition he saw to the baggage train when on the march, commanded the artillery during battle and supervised weapons training in peacetime (Vegetius 2.9). A career soldier, this senior officer provided a degree of professionalism and continuity, which the two senatorial officers might seem to lack.

Immediately below the *praefectus castrorum* ranked the five equestrian tribunes. An equestrian tribune held no independent command in the legion, but from at least the Flavian era onwards it was customary to already have experienced leadership as a commander of an *auxilia* unit and thus to be in a position to offer (if asked) the legate some practical advice on the handling and disposition of auxiliary forces in his command area. Equally, the tribune would have the chance to see a legion in action from within, which would stand him in good stead when (or if) he went on to further commands. In peacetime, for instance, his duties mainly centred on camp security, physical training and overseeing of the stores and medical facilities.

Centuriate

Tacitus informs us that during the Rhine mutiny the legionaries had turned against their centurions and given them each 60 strokes of the lash, 'one for each centurion in the legion' (*Annales* 1.32.1). Likewise the six centurions of each cohort still retained their old republican titles: *pilus prior* and *pilus posterior*, *princeps prior* and *princeps posterior*, and *hastatus prior* and *hastatus posterior*. These titles obviously reflect their former positions in the tripartite battle-lines of the Republic: *pilani* (*triarii*), *principes* and *hastati*. It is generally believed that the centurions of *cohors X* were junior to those of *cohors VIIII*, and so on, so that promotion could consist of a transfer to a cohort of a lower number. At the same time, the senior centurion of each cohort was the *pilus prior*, followed by the *princeps prior* and *hastatus prior*, then by the three posterior centurions in the same order. The most important duty of the centurions was, of course, the command of their own century, and, if promoted to be *pilus prior*, the command of the cohort in which they held that post.

In the *cohors prima*, with the introduction of the five double-strength centuries, the titles were *primus pilus*, *princeps prior*, *hastatus prior*, *princeps posterior* and *hastatus posterior*; collectively they were known as the *primi ordines* ('the front rankers') and enjoyed immense prestige. Even more so the *primus pilus*, who, as the legion's top soldier, commanded the first century of the first cohort and had charge of the eagle-standard. As in Caesar's day the post was normally a one-year appointment, but under the Principate it automatically elevated the holder to the equestrian order. Invariably, therefore, a *primus pilus* went on to become *praefectus castrorum*, his last post before retirement.

Petronius Fortunatus, who probably came from Africa, saw five decades of service in the army. He was a ranker for four years in *I Italica* stationed in Moesia Inferior. He was then promoted to the rank of centurion and served as such in no fewer than 13 legions, including those stationed in Syria Palestina (where he probably met his wife in Jerusalem, then a Roman colony under the name of Aelia Capitolina), Numidia and the provinces along the Danube and the Rhine, receiving decorations in one of the Parthian campaigns, possibly that under Marcus Aurelius, yet never entering the *primi ordines* and so not attaining the coveted post of *primus pilus*. Nonetheless Fortunatus' career is proudly recorded on his tombstone, which was found near Cillium in Africa. The inscription runs as follows:

[Petronius Fortunatus] served for 50 years, four in *legio I Ita[lica]* as clerk (*librarius*), officer in charge of watchword (*tesserarius*), second-in-command of a century (*optio*), standard-bearer (*signifer*); he was promoted to centurion (*centurio*) by vote of the [same] legion, served as centurion of *legio I Ital[ica]*, centurion of *legio VI F[errata]*, centurion of *legio I Min[ervia]*, centurion *legio X Gem[ina]*, centurion of *legio II A[ugusta]*, centurion of *legio III A[ugusta]*, centurion of *legio III Gall[ica]*, centurion of *legio XXX Ulp[ia]*, centurion of *legio VI Vic[trix]*, centurion of *legio III Cyr[enaica]*, centurion of *legio XV Apol[linaris]*, centurion of *legio II Par[thica]*, centurion of *legio I Adiutrix*; in the Parthian expedition he was decorated for bravery with a *corona muralis* and *corona vallaris* and with torques and *phalerae*; he was in his 80th year at the completion of this monument for himself and for Claudia Marcia Capitolina, his beloved wife, who was in her 65th year at the time of the completion of this monument, and for his son Marcus Petronius Fortunatus, who served in the army for six years, centurion of *legio XXII Primig[enia]*, centurion of *legio II A[ugusta]*, lived 35 years; for their beloved son, Fortunatus and Marcia, his parents, built this as a memorial.
ILS 2658

Monumentul de la Adamklissi, metope XXVIII (Istanbul, Arkeoloji Müzesi, 1434 T). Here we see two bareheaded and unarmoured legionaries dressed in tunics and wearing *focalis*. The wearing of the *gladius*, with its distinctive pommel and handgrip, high on the left hip, the orthodox position, suggests they are centurions.
(akg-images/Erich Lessing)

The two *coronae* called *muralis* and *vallaris*, both of which were gold, appear commonly in inscriptions, and in origin the first was awarded to the first man over the wall of a besieged town and the second for the first man over the enemy's rampart. The *phalerae* were embossed discs, usually of silver with gold inlay, attached to the corselet by a leather harness. Despite his obvious courage, however, promotion within the centurionate came slowly, and in each successive step it looks as if Fortunatus changed his legion. This may explain why the peripatetic

The Hutcheson Hill distance slab (No. 11), Antonine Wall (Glasgow, Hunterian Museum). In the centre panel a laurel wreath is placed on the beak of the *aquila* of *legio XX Valeria Victrix* by the personification of Victory. Meanwhile, two bound captives watch on. (Fields-Carré Collection)

Fortunatus, who even ended up in Britannia on two separate postings, never reached the top of his career.

Though men from outside the army could be directly commissioned to a post in the centurionate, as was Fortunatus' 29-year old son Marcus, most centurions rose from the ranks and since Marius the legions were recruited from the *proletarii*. Yet a centurion was still responsible for the administration of his century, for the conveyance of orders, the leadership of his men in battle and for training and maintaining discipline. On average a man of reasonable literacy and good conduct could reach the centurionate, which covered all the lower and middle-ranking officers of the army, in 15 to 20 years. Fortunatus himself, having first served as a clerk, was manifestly literate and had some knowledge of arithmetic.

Occasionally centurions were chosen by popular vote, as was Fortunatus. However, this method of promotion could be a risky one in certain circumstances, and Tacitus records (*Historiae* 3.49.2) how M. Antonius Primus, after the Flavian success at Second Cremona, gave his legions the right of appointing new centurions to replace those who had been killed. This was a time of civil war, and it comes as little surprise to learn that the most undisciplined candidates were elected.

Junior officers

Each *centurio* was assisted by a second-in-command, an *optio*, so named because under the Republic *centuriones* 'adopted' their own *optiones* (*adoptandum*, Varro *de Lingua Latina* 5.91, Festus 201.23), a standard-bearer (*signifer*), a musician (*cornicen*) and a guard commander (*tesserarius*). The *optio*, who would take command if the *centurio* fell, traditionally stood at the rear of the *centuria*, while the *tesserarius* supervised the posting of the sentries at night and was responsible for distributing the following day's watchword, which he received each night inscribed on a wooden tablet (*tessera*). The *signiferi* ranked with *optiones* as *principales*, receiving double the pay of a legionary, and among their duties was to keep the pay and savings accounts of their *centuria*.

Each *centuria* carried a standard (*signum*) basically consisting of an assemblage of discs (*phalerae*) mounted on a pole surmounted by a spear point or effigy hand, below which could be an inscribed tablet indicating the number of the *cohors* the *centuria* belonged to (e.g. COH(ors) V). As no more than six *phalerae* seem to be placed on any one *signum* in the many illustrations of them on coins and sculptures, it has been suggested that the number of discs denotes the number of the century in its cohort.

The eagle-standard (*aquila*) was carried into battle by a senior standard-bearer, the *aquilifer*, second only to a centurion in rank. It was under the personal care of the *primus pilus*. While its safe custody was equivalent to the continuance of the legion as a fighting unit, however depleted in numbers, its loss brought the greatest ignominy on any survivors and could result in the disbandment of the legion in disgrace. For example, at the start of his reign Vespasianus disbanded four Rhine legions (*I Germanica, IIII Macedonica, XV Primigenia* and *XVI Gallica*), disgraced for having either surrendered or lost their eagles during the rebellion of Iulius Civilis, and in their place, according to Cassius Dio (55.24.3), raised two new legions, using two of the numbers of those he had just axed and presumably some of their personnel as well (*IIII Flavia felix* and *XVI Flavia firma*). Velleius Paterculus (2.97.1), who served under Prince Tiberius in Germania as a *praefectus equitum*, then in Pannonia as a *legatus Augusti legionis*, reports the loss of its eagle-standard by the famed *V Alaudae*, recently transferred from Iberia to the Rhine, where it was part of the army of M. Lollius defeated by the Germanic Sugambri in 17 BC. Likewise, Suetonius says (*Vespasianus* 4.4) *XII Fulminata*, another illustrious Caesarian formation, lost its eagle in Iudaea under C. Cestius Gallus in AD 66. However, it is interesting to note that these particular losses did not lead to the legions being disbanded.

The eagle itself, initially of silver but later of gold (or perhaps silver-gilt), was customarily depicted with a golden thunderbolt gripped in its talons, its wings outstretched and its head cast forward, displaying its readiness for flight on orders from Iuppiter. Little wonder, therefore, the legionary regarded his legion standard with appreciable awe. We need only to recall the special campaign launched across the Rhine by Germanicus in order to avenge the tragic defeat of Varus and recover the lost standards.

Backing disc of an *imago imperatoris* from Newstead-Trimontium (Edinburgh, National Museums of Scotland), which once bore an image of the reigning emperor with solar crown. Mounted on a pole and carried by an *imaginifer*, this standard served as a reminder to the soldiers of their oath and loyalty to their commander-in-chief. (Fields-Carré Collection)

Each *turma* had its standard carried by a *signifer*. Here the well-known example from Hexham Abbey of Flavianus, a *signifer* of *ala Petriana*, a unit once stationed at Corbridge-Coria and later at Stanwix near Carlisle. He carries a *signum* that looks like a large medallion. Note the plumes adorning his helmet. (Fields-Carré Collection)

During the Principate the portrait of the reigning emperor (*imago imperatoris*) was also carried by each legion. Reminding the soldiers of their loyalty and devotion, this standard was carried on a separate pole by the *imaginifer*. Tacitus (*Annales* 1.39.4) clearly implies that the *imago* shared the same honours as the *aquila*, and it too was under the personal care of the *primus pilus*. As well as bringing the emperor into a closer relationship with his soldiers, the *imago* became of increasing significance with the rise and fall of dynasties. Thus when the emperor's portrait was torn down from the *imagines*, it was a sign of military revolt. When the Vitellian commander A. Caecina Alienus succeeded in winning over some of his army to the cause of Vespasianus while the rest were away on routine duties, the soldiers signified the change by tearing down the portraits of Vitellius and taking an oath to Vespasianus. But when the rest of the soldiers returned to camp and saw Vitellius' portraits had been torn down and Vespasianus' name written up, they were stunned. Once they realized what had happened, they refused to accept the change of allegiance, set up Vitellius' portraits again and put Caecina under arrest (Tacitus *Historiae* 3.13–14).

The early Christian writer Tertullian (fl. AD 200) says the religious system of the Roman Army 'is entirely devoted to the worship of the standards' (*Apologia* 16.8). Though this is somewhat of an exaggeration, Tertullian was not completely wrong in his judgement. The cultivation of *esprit de corps* is a necessity for any military unit, and for this purpose the cult of the standards was ideal. In a very real sense, the standards formed the very identity of the unit to which they belonged and thus were revered as sacred objects. As his soldiers commenced their advance into contact at the battle of Idistaviso, Germanicus, according to Tacitus, took the sudden appearance of eight eagles as a good omen, 'the legions' own special guiding spirit' (*Annales* 2.17.2).

Finally in a legionary headquarters there was a junior officer known as a *cornicularius*. Named for a decoration of two small horns hanging from his helmet, the *cornicularius* was responsible for the staff of clerks (*librarii*) that formed the record-office (*tabularium*). Here you would have found clerks with special duties, such as the *librarius horreorum* who kept the granary records, the *librarius depositorum* who collected the soldiers' savings, and the *librarius caducorum*, who secured the belongings of those killed in action. As in a modern army, the Roman Army of the Principate generated a mountain of paperwork. Thus a recruit who possessed writing and numeric skills would probably stand a good chance of appointment as *librarius* (Vegetius 2.19). As we know, centurion Fortunatus started his long army career not as a *miles* but as a *librarius*, and a letter written in March AD 107 reveals how another recruit came to be a *librarius*. Iulius Apollinaris writes in his native Greek to his father back home in Egypt:

> I'm getting on all right. Thanks to Serapis I got here safely, and so far I haven't been caught by any fatigues like cutting building-stones. In fact, I went up to Claudius Severus, *legatus Augusti pro praetore*, and asked him to make me a *librarius* on his own staff. He said, 'There's no vacancy at present, but I'll make you a *librarius legionis* for the time being, with hopes of promotion.' So I went straight from the general to the *cornicularius*.
> *P. Mich.* VIII 466.18–32

Our young soldier was serving in newly annexed Arabia, and a contingent of his legion (*VI Ferrata fidelis constans*) was obviously employed in the local quarries. His status as a *librarius* made him an *immunis*, and thus he was exempt from the backbreaking bore of stone breaking.

Equestrian officers

While the senatorial families, previously the dominant force in Rome, might resent the changes wrought by Augustus, and look back with nostalgia at the old Republic, for many Romans the Principate was the opening of political opportunities. This applied in particular to members of the equestrian order.

It seems likely that a legionary legate had overall command over the *auxilia* units attached to his legion. We know that in Britannia the eight *cohortes* of Batavi were attached to *legio XIIII Gemina*, and were to depart with it in AD 66 as part of Nero's planned expedition to the Caucasus, which never materialized (Tacitus *Historiae* 1.6.4, 2.27.2, 4.15.1). Auxiliary commanders themselves, however, were drawn solely from the equestrian order. Be that as it may, many of these units were still commanded by 'native leaders', some even of 'royal stock', such as the Batavian noble Flavius Cerialis, *praefectus* of *cohors VIIII Batavorum* at Vindolanda in the years around AD 100 (e.g. *Tab. Vindol.* II 238, 250).

From the Flavians onwards these commanders were ranked as follows: *praefectus cohortis* (*cohors peditata quingenaria*), *tribunus cohortis* (*cohors peditata milliaria*) and *praefectus equitum* (*ala quingenaria* and *ala milliaria*). Thus cavalry commanders were men at the peak of what was known as the *tres militiae*, equestrian officers who had already served as prefects of *cohortes quingenariae* and either as tribunes in legions (*tribuni angusticlavii*) or tribunes of *cohortes milliariae* (*CIL* 2.2637, cf. Suetonius *Divus Claudius* 25.1). By the 2nd century AD there were some 90 posts as *praefectus equitum* (now known as *praefectus alae*), and the commands of the *alae milliariae* devolved on a select group of about ten consisting of the pick of the men who had already commanded *alae quingenariae*. But the pinnacle of equestrian achievement did not end here.

The province of Egypt was organized differently from all other provinces. It was the emperor's private possession, and no senator was allowed to set foot in it without his authority. Consequently there could be no *legatus Augusti pro praetore* or *legati Augusti legionis* in the province, and, while the governor was called a *praefectus Aegypto*, the commanders of the legions in the province had the title of *praefecti legionum*. These *praefecti* were all men of equestrian rank. A senator in such a province might harbour dangerous, 'republican' ambitions; as well as its garrison of two legions, there were a further four legions in Syria. There is some justification for such a view in Tacitus (*Historiae* 1.11.1) who thought that Augustus wished to control tightly a province, which was populous, wealthy and fertile. So what was once Cleopatra's Egypt became the crown of an equestrian career.

Finally, as the *primus pilus* received the rank of an equestrian, it was possible for him to continue his army career by obtaining an independent command in the *auxilia* if he so wished, thereby taking the successive steps *praefectus cohortis*, *tribunus legionis* or *tribunus cohortis*, and *praefectus equitum*. On the other hand, he could opt for a more glamorous posting and serve in the garrison troops of Rome as a tribune in the watch (*vigiles*), seven cohorts responsible for policing and fire-fighting, the urban cohorts (*cohortes urbanae*), three (later seven) in number, or the praetorian guard itself. A very few went on to equestrian governorships.

Command and control in action

The tradition of the Republic had been that a senator should be prepared to serve the state in whatever capacity it demanded, and be proficient. A practical people, the Romans believed that the man chosen by the competent authority would be up to the task in hand. In the Republic that authority had been the electorate, under the Principate it would be the emperor. In other words there was no training for the job. Thus the man sent to command an army would have to learn the skills himself, from the leisure of reading books or the harder lesson of the battlefield.

It is interesting that handbooks on military tactics and the art of generalship continued to be written under the emperors, notably by Onasander (under Claudius), Frontinus (under Domitianus), Aelian (under Traianus), Arrian (under Hadrianus) and Polyainos (under Antonius Pius). All these authors claimed to be writing with a principal purpose, namely to elucidate military matters for the benefit of army commanders, and even the emperor himself. Thus Frontinus, in the prologue of the *Strategemata*, explains his intentions:

> For in this way army commanders will be equipped with examples of good planning and foresight, and this will develop their own ability to think out and carry into effect similar operations. An added benefit

Tombstone of Aurelius Surus, dated AD 210–15 (Istanbul, Arkeoloji Müzesi, 5826 T). He was a *bucinator* in *legio I Adiutrix pia fidelis*; having served for 18 years he died age 40. The memorial was put up by his comrade and heir, Septimius Vibianus, a fellow Syrian. In his right hand Surus holds the tool of his trade, the *bucina* or trumpet. (Fields-Carré Collection)

will be the commander will not be worried about the outcome of his own stratagem when he compares it with innovations already tested in practice.
Frontinus *Strategemata* 1 *praefatio*

As under the Republic, the emperors saw no need to establish a system to train future commanders. On the contrary, it was still believed that by using handbooks and taking advice, a man of average ability could direct a Roman army (Campbell 1996: 325–31).

Traditionally the Romans had an organized but uncomplicated approach to tactics. The principles were: the use of cavalry for flank attacks and encirclement; the placing of a force in reserve; the deployment of a battle line that could maintain contact, readiness to counterattack, flexibility in the face of unexpected enemy manoeuvres. As the disposition of forces and the tactical placing of reserves were vital elements of generalship, the Roman commander needed to be in a position from where he could see the entire battle. The underlying rationale of this style of generalship is well expressed by Onasander when he says the general 'can aid his army far less by fighting than he can harm it if he should be killed, since the knowledge of a general is far more important than his physical strength' (*Stratêgikos* 33.1). To have the greatest influence on the battle the general should stay close to, but behind his fighting line, directing and encouraging his men from this relatively safe position.

This was certainly what Antonius Primus did at Second Cremona (AD 69). In bright moonlight the Flavian commander rode around urging his men on, 'some by taunts and appeals to their pride, many by praise and encouragement, all by hope and promises' (Tacitus *Historia* 3.24.1). That other renowned Flavian general, Q. Petilius Cerialis, is depicted during the rebellion of Civilis (AD 70) doing the same thing, which occasioned no small risk (ibid. 4.77.2).

During his governorship of Cappadocia, Arrian had to repel an invasion of the Alani. Arrian wrote an account of the preparatory dispositions he made for

A fragmentary tombstone from Chesterholm-Vindolanda. Its inscription tells us that Titus Annius, a legionary centurion (*centurio legionis*) serving as the acting-commander of *cohors I Tungrorum* based at Vindolanda, may have been a casualties of a revolt (*inbell*[o ... *inter*]*fectvs*) that flared in Britannia at the time of Hadrianus' succession. (Fields-Carré Collection)

this campaign, the *Ektaxis katà Alanon*. This unique work, in which the author represents himself as the famous Athenian soldier-scholar Xenophon, sets out the commands of the governor as if he were actually giving them. He had two legions, *XII Fulminata* and *XV Apollinaris*, and a number of *auxilia* units under his command, in all some 20,000 men. Arrian himself took charge of the dispositions and recognized the need for personal, hands-on leadership:

Ti. Claudius Nero (42 BC–AD 37)
Tiberius was the eldest son of Livia by her first husband, Ti. Claudius Nero. He thus came from a noble family much distinguished in republican times, a time when such a man could expect high office because of his military achievements alone. For Tiberius it was not to be, and as the years passed he would become darker and more morose. For instance, at Augustus' insistence he divorced Vipsania Agrippina, daughter of Agrippa and Caecilia Attica, and married Iulia, daughter of Augustus and Agrippa's widow, in 11 BC. He seems to have been genuinely fond of Vipsania, whom he had married in 19 BC, and would come to regret bitterly his loveless marriage to the headstrong Iulia.

Outside of the traumas of family life Tiberius was to enjoy a successful military career. In 15 BC, along with his younger brother Nero Claudius Drusus, with whom he shared a natural propensity for warfare, he had campaigned in the region between the Alps and the Danube, and after Drusus' death in 9 BC, was active on the Rhine. Consul in 13 BC (with Varus as colleague), and again in 7 BC when he also received an award of *triumphalia* and a second *imperator* acclamation, he held the *tribunicia potestas* for five years in 6 BC, a clear sign of Augustus' approval. Yet he chose to retire in dudgeon to

Rhodes, apparently protesting against Augustus' blatant dynastic promotion of his own grandsons (and adopted sons), the sons of Iulia and Agrippa. According to Suetonius (*Tiberius* 10.1), however, Tiberius retired to Rhodes in order to prevent his own prestige standing in the way of the public careers of Caius and Lucius Caesar – palace machinations or was Tiberius retiring hurt?

It appears that though Augustus, after the death of Agrippa, trusted Tiberius with the important military commands, the emperor did not favour his stepson as a successor. Thus Augustus sent Iulia a decree of divorce in Tiberius' name in 2 BC, and the following year Tiberius' *tribunicia potestas* expired and was not renewed. He was only allowed to return to Rome as a private citizen (*privatus*) after urging by Livia and the agreement of Caius Caesar in AD 2.

Finally in AD 4, after the untimely death of Caius Caesar (Lucius had expired two years beforehand), Tiberius, now 45 years of age, was adopted (with Agrippa Postumus) as Augustus' son, and granted *tribunicia potestas* for ten years. However, he was in turn obliged to adopt his nephew Germanicus, even though he had a natural son, Drusus minor, probably only two years younger. In the same year he was back on the Rhine to renew the German campaign, and two years later, in AD 6, he was, with Germanicus, sent to deal with the Pannonian revolt. It took the greater part of three years, with much hard fighting, to put down this terrifying uprising. Almost immediately news was received of the Varian disaster, so Tiberius was hurriedly dispatched to the Rhine with all available troops transferred from other provinces to reinforce his army. But the expected Germanic invasion did not materialize, and so Tiberius mounted punitive expeditions beyond the Rhine to restore the name of Rome. In AD 11 Germanicus joined him in this arduous task.

As he grew old and weak, Augustus sought to prevent any power vacuum on his death. In AD 13 Tiberius became de facto co-emperor after being given a further grant of *tribunicia potestas* for ten years and an *imperium* the equal of

Augustus'. The following year, on the death of Augustus, oaths of loyalty were given to him. Tiberius was a tragic figure. He was an outstanding military commander – the best of his age – but he was neither interested in nor fitted for the intrigue and politics of Rome. He was in his true element on campaign with his soldiers, but because of his birth, he was doomed to become emperor.

Tiberius was stern, cold, reserved and formal with a strong sense of duty. He was a bold leader in the field, as his successful campaigns across the Rhine demonstrated, with a real talent for soldiering. He was popular and diligent, often spending the day in the saddle and the night under the stars, sitting at the table to eat his meals instead of reclining on a couch, or even squatting on the bare earth. He was careful to look after the sick and preserve his soldiers from unnecessary losses in battle. It was an established literary topos for a 'good' general to share his soldiers' privations and lead from the front, a theme we shall come across repeatedly when we look at the lives of other Roman commanders. Yet the 'Napoleonic' euphoria of his soldiers when Tiberius returned to command them was doubtless genuine (Velleius Paterculus 2.104.4).

Tiberius' great flaw was that he was deeply suspicious of others, to the point of paranoia. Though intelligent and shrewd, he was easily hurt and could be cold-bloodedly vengeful. He knew Augustus favoured others over him and that he was the eighth choice in his succession plans. Rumour blamed his mother, Livia, whom Caligula later dubbed 'Ulysses in a frock' (Suetonius *Caius* 23.2), for the premature deaths of the other imperial candidates (the picture popularized by Robert Graves with a little help from Tacitus). Whatever the truth of the matter, she was determined that her son should succeed, but he was unenthusiastic about becoming emperor and ended by loathing his position.

The commander of the entire army, Xenophon [i.e. Arrian], should lead from a position well in front of the infantry standards; he should visit all the ranks and examine how they have been drawn up; he should bring order to those who are in disarray and praise those who are properly drawn up.
Arrian *Ektaxis* 10

To carry out his orders Arrian could look to the legionary legate (one of the *legati legionis* seems to be absent), the military tribunes, centurions and decurions. Nonetheless, it is interesting to note that the tactics advocated by Arrian are safe and simple, competent rather than brilliant.

Of all the senior officers listed above, it was the centurions that were the key to an army's success in battle. Centurions were a strongly conservative group who had a vital role to play in preserving the discipline and organization of the army and providing continuity of command. Yet they owed their position of command and respect to their own bravery and effectiveness in combat, and when they stood on the field of battle they were directly responsible for leading their men forwards. Thus their understanding of an intended battle plan was vital for success simply because they were the ones commanding the men on the ground.

The *aquilifer* played an important if comparatively minor leadership role in battle too. He was, after all, the man who served as a rallying point during the chaos of battle, and could urge hesitant soldiers forwards during a particularly dangerous moment. C. Suetonius Paulinus had formed his army up opposite Mona (Anglesey) ready to assault, but his soldiers wavered at the eerie spectacle of incanting Druids and frenzied women on the shoreline. They were spurred into action, however, when 'onward pressed their standards' (Tacitus *Annales* 14.30.2). When we consider the singular value the soldiers placed on their *aquila* and how its loss to the enemy would mean a permanent stain on the honour of their unit, it comes as no surprise to learn that some sacrificed themselves in its defence. At Second Cremona the *aquila* of *VII Galbiana* was only saved after 'Atilius Verus' desperate execution upon the enemy and at the cost, finally of his own life' (Tacitus *Historiae* 3.22.3). L. Atilius Verus, once a centurion of *V Macedonica*, was *primus pilus* of the rookie *VII Galbiana*.

Closely associated with the standards was the *cornicen*, a junior officer who blew the *cornu*, a bronze tube bent into almost a full circle with a transverse bar to strengthen it. Another instrument was the *tuba*, a straight trumpet, played by the *tubicen*. Music was used for sleep, reveille and the changing of the guard (Frontinus *Strategemata* 1.1.9, Josephus *Bellum Iudaicum* 3.86), but its main function was tactical. Therefore on the battlefield itself different calls, accompanied by visual signals such as the raising of the standards, would sound the alarm or order a recall (Tacitus *Annales* 1.28.3, 68.3). Naturally, when the troops charged into contact and raised their war cry (*clamor*), the *cornicines* and *tubicines* blew their instruments so as to encourage their comrades and discourage the enemy.

The Roman Army in battle

Surprising as it may seem, there is no history of the Roman Army by any ancient author and little detailed examination of military practices. Among the Roman historians Tacitus has some detached references to the arms and equipment of legionaries and auxiliaries, and to formations adopted by such generals as Cn. Domitius Corbulo and Cn. Iulius Agricola. It is indeed curious that Joseph ben Matthias, better known to history as Josephus (T. Flavius Iosephus), wrote the best descriptions of the army in war and peace. An aristocratic priest chosen by the Sanhedrin, the Jewish council of state, to defend Galilee in the revolt of AD 66 against Rome, Josephus witnessed firsthand the legions of Vespasianus and his son Titus in action against his Jewish countrymen. Like Polybios before him, as a defeated foreigner Josephus was very much interested in seeking what were the primary factors that contributed to the superiority of Roman arms.

Roman tactical doctrine and practice

'It would not be far from the truth to call their drills bloodless battle, their battles bloody drills' (*Bellum Iudaicum* 3.75), so runs the most celebrated line of Josephus. The patriot-turned-partisan presents a rather idealized view of the Roman Army's efficiency, but he is not far wrong when he puts his failure down to the effectiveness of the arduous training given to the legions. The legionary had to be both physically and mentally stronger than his 'barbarian' adversary. As Josephus points out, 'military exercises give the Roman soldiers not only tough bodies but determined spirits too' (ibid. 3.102). Training brought not only efficiency and effectiveness but also discipline and confidence, or in Varro's very apt dictionary definition: 'Army (*exercitus*), because it is made better by means of exercise (*exercitando*).'

Although a battle fought between the armies of Otho and Vitellius, rivals for the imperial purple, Tacitus' description of First Cremona is well worth a look at:

42. At this moment, the enemy [i.e. the Vitellians] advanced with unbroken ranks. In fighting qualities and numbers he had the advantage. As for the Othonians, scattered, outnumbered and weary as they were, they went into action gallantly. Indeed, as the battle was fought over a wide area thickly planted with a maze of vines and vine-props, it presented a variety of aspects. The two sides made contact at long and short range, in loose or compact formation. On the high road, Vitellians and Othonians fought hand-to-hand, throwing the weight of their bodies and shield-bosses (*umbonis*) against each other. The usual discharge of *pila* was scrapped, and swords (*gladii*) and axes (*secures*) used to pierce helmets and armour. Knowing each other [i.e. the praetorians and *legio I Italica*] and watched by their comrades, they fought the fight that was to settle the whole campaign.

43. As it turned out, two legions made contact in open country between the Padus [Po] and the road [Via Postumia]. They were Vitellian *legio XXI Fulminata*, long known and famous, and on the Othonian side *legio I Adiutrix*, which had never fought before, but was in high spirits and avid of distinction in its first action. *Legio I Adiutrix* overran the front ranks of *legio XXI Fulminata*, and carried off their eagle (*aquila*). Smarting under this humiliation, the latter got their own back by charging *legio I Adiutrix*, who lost their legate, Orfidius Benignus, and a great number of standards

(*signa*) and flags (*vexilla*). In another part of the field, *legio V* [*Alaudae*] punished *legio XIII* [*Gemina*], while the *vexillatio* from *legio XIIII* [*Gemina Martia Victrix*] was outnumbered and rolled up. Long after the Othonian commanders had fled, Caecina and Valens [i.e. the Vitellian commanders] were still bringing up reinforcements to strengthen their men. Then, at the eleventh hour, came the Batavi [*cohortes*], after routing the force of gladiators. These had crossed the Padus in their ships only to be done to death in the very water by the *cohortes* confronting them. As a sequel to this success, the Batavi now delivered their onslaught on the Othonian flank.
Tacitus *Historiae* 2.42–43

When Roman armies were pitted against each other we might expect sophisticated tactics skilfully applied. But Tacitus' brief but dramatic account tells us this was far from the case. Roman tactics were basically aggressive, with the doctrine of the offensive dominant. This did not make the Romans invincible – as we shall see they were to suffer terrible reverses – but they believed that defeat in one battle did not mean defeat in war.

Legion

For the first century of the Principate we possess no order of battle with a detailed description of the dispositions adopted, but Tacitus' account of Domitius Corbulo's campaigns against Parthia suggests that matters on the field of battle were very much the same as in Caesar's day. In one of his encounters with the Parthian king Tiridates in AD 58, Domitius Corbulo placed the *auxilia* on the flanks and *legio VI Ferrata*, reinforced with 3,000 men from *III Gallica* to give the impression of strength, in the centre (Tacitus *Annales* 13.38.6). For the legion, therefore, a favourite battle formation would be the triple line of cohorts, *triplex acies*. As we shall see, the double line, *duplex acies*, is attested too, and the very flexibility of the cohort structure with its sub-divisions of *centuriae* and *contubernia* would allow almost any variation. Even so, the cohort was to remain the basic tactical unit and the century the basic administrative unit.

In his description of the defeat of Boudica at Mancetter (AD 61), Cassius Dio picks out the contrast between the contending sides:

> Thereupon the armies approached each other, the barbarians with much shouting, mingled with menacing battle songs, but the Romans silently and in order until they came within a javelin [*akóntion* in Dio's Greek] throw of the enemy. Then, while their foes were still advancing against them at a walk, the Romans rushed forward at a signal and charged at full speed, and when the clash came, easily broke through the opposing ranks.
> Cassius Dio 62.12.1–2

Silently executed, the Roman advance was a slow, steady affair, culminating in a close-range barrage of *pila* and an explosive charge of armoured men. The enemy often gave way very quickly, as did our front-rank Britons at Mancetter. Similarly, in AD 14 Germanicus led *XXI Rapax* in an assault, which swiftly scattered the Germans in a single, decisive charge (Tacitus *Annales* 1.51.2).

Our legionary was above all a trained swordsman, and had been since the days of Marius (Fields 2008: 37–42). Tacitus and Vegetius lay great stress on the *gladius* being employed by the legionary for thrusting rather than slashing. As Vegetius rightly

'Sword of Tiberius' (London, British Museum, GR 1866 8-6.1). Found in the Rhine at Mainz, this is another example of the long-pointed 'Mainz'-type *gladius*. So-called because its scabbard bears a relief of Tiberius receiving Germanicus in AD 17 on his 'heroic' return to Rome following his Germanic campaigns. (© The Trustees of the British Museum)

says, 'a slash-cut, whatever its force, seldom kills' (1.12), and thus a thrust was certainly more likely to deliver the fatal wound. Having thrown the *pilum* and charged into contact, the standard drill for the legionary was to punch the enemy in the face with the shield-boss and then jab him in the belly with the razor-sharp point of the sword. The use of the thrust also meant the legionary kept most of his torso well covered, and was thus protected, by the *scutum*.

In his version of Mancetter, Tacitus has the Roman commander C. Suetonius Paulinus delivering a pre-battle speech in which he instructs his legionaries to knock over the Britons by punching them with their shields and then to jab them with their swords. In other words, he is reminding them that they have three offensive weapons, *pilum*, *scutum* and *gladius*: 'Just keep in close order. Throw your javelins (*pila*), and then carry on: use your shield-bosses (*umbonis*) to fell them, swords (*gladii*) to kill them. Do not think of plunder. When you have won, you will have everything' (*Annales* 14.36.3).

The Adamklissi monument (Metope xviii) shows a legionary punching an opponent's face with the boss of his *scutum*, thereby unbalancing him, and jabbing him in the belly with his *gladius*. Here the *gladius* is being used primarily in an upward thrust directed from below the *scutum*, the legionary getting under the opponent's attack and penetrating his lower stomach or groin, the soft, fleshy parts below the ribcage. A thrust would kill for sure only if it penetrated the internal organs, not when it jammed against a bone. However, penetration wounds to these exposed lower areas were almost always fatal, leading in a few days, if not hours, to an agonizing death from shock, peritonitis or other infections, as the contents of the intestines spilled out into the abdominal cavity and the victim shrank from blood and fluid loss.

Auxiliaries

The *auxilia* were a cheaper and, given their primary organization at a lower level (i.e. *cohortes* for infantry and *alae* for cavalry), more flexible way of providing the army with the manpower to fulfil its role, especially along the frontiers of the empire. To the *auxilia* fell the tasks of patrolling, containing raids, tax collecting and the multitudinous duties of frontier troops – the legions were stationed within the frontiers, both to act as a strategic reserve and to intimidate potentially rebellious indigenous 'friendlies'.

As noted, when it came to large-scale actions a favourite formation for the legion was the *triplex acies*. The *auxilia cohortes*, meanwhile, would be stationed on either side of a centre formed by the legions, and *alae* deployed on the wings with an additional force kept in reserve. This was the formation, albeit without the luxury of reserve *alae*, adopted by Suetonius Paulinus against Boudica (Tacitus *Annales* 14.37). Alternatively, the *cohortes* could form the first line and be supported by the legions, as did Agricola at Mons Graupius. Again *alae* formed the wings, but here they were supported by more *alae* behind the main battle line (Tacitus *Agricola* 35.2, 37.2).

Although there were specialist units of archers and slingers, it would be wrong to view the infantryman of the *auxilia* as some form of light infantry. Weighed down with helmet, body armour, sword, spear and shield, this equipment is not that of a nimble skirmisher. On the contrary, they formed the first line at Idistaviso (AD 16) and Vetera (AD 70), operated in close-order using the

Monumentul de la Adamklissi, dedicated to Mars Ultor, the Avenger, was probably the handiwork of soldiers. This is metope I (Adamklissi, Muzeul de Archeologie), which depicts a cavalryman charging into battle, his *lancea* held horizontally in a relaxed position. The trooper wears a short-sleeved mail-shirt and carries a hexagonal *clipeus* but, curiously, is bareheaded. (Fields-Carré Collection)

Nero Claudius Germanicus Caesar (15 BC–AD 19)

Nero Claudius Drusus, brother of the future emperor Tiberius, married Antonia minor, the younger daughter of the great Marcus Antonius and Augustus' sister, Octavia. Much like her father, Antonia was a strong willed and independent woman, widely respected and admired. She bore her husband three children, Germanicus (the father of Caligula), Claudius (the future emperor) and Livia Iulia (destined to become the mistress of the sinister Sejanus). By the same token her husband was the darling of the people, a talented general who, unlike his elder brother, oozed charm and cordiality, who in a series of brilliant campaigns between 12 and 9 BC, had carried Roman arms as far as the Elbe. His death in 9 BC, after a fall from a horse, plunged Rome into deepest mourning. He was honoured by the posthumous title of Germanicus, which passed on to his eldest son.

Obviously Drusus' unexpected death prevented him from consolidating his victories, and his place in Germania was eventually to be taken by Germanicus, whose charm far exceeded his talents, and whose popularity with the people would outstrip even his father's. Suetonius claims (*Caius* 3.1) that he surpassed his contemporaries both in physical and moral qualities, while Tacitus (*Annales* 2.72.1) goes as far as to compare his tragic hero with Alexander the Great, saying that if he had ruled he would have outdone him in military achievements just as he surpassed him in

personal qualities. These impressions clearly represent a romanticized view of Germanicus, one that was no doubt fostered by anti-Tiberian elements after his early demise. Indeed, many believed that Tiberius, jealous of the ever-popular Germanicus, had a hand in his death.

As a clear indication of Augustus' determination to be succeeded by someone from his own line, Germanicus, shortly after his adoption by Tiberius, was married to the emperor's granddaughter Agrippina major. From this union would spring two future emperors, Caligula, the youngest of their three sons, and Nero, the son of their eldest daughter Agrippina minor. Germanicus himself first achieved distinction serving under his uncle (now adoptive father) Tiberius during the Pannonian revolt, where he showed courage and military skill. Five years later, in AD 11, he went to Germania to join Tiberius once again.

He was consul in AD 12, and the following year was granted *imperium pro consule* by Augustus at the time of Tiberius' elevation to co-emperor. At this time he was also given overall authority over the eight legions and supporting *auxilia* posted on the Rhine. His mettle was soon to be put to the test. On the death of Augustus he was faced with a serious mutiny of the four legions (*I Germanica*, *V Alaudae*, *XX* and *XXI Rapax*) in Germania Inferior, where riots had broken out and discipline had collapsed, with centurions being seized and flogged. When he reached the camp Germanicus tried to appeal to the men's loyalty. His efforts failed, and making a histrionic threat to commit suicide he was jokingly encouraged to see it through. In the end he was reduced to producing a forged letter of Tiberius supposedly offering concessions, and to dipping into the cash he carried for official expenses. The hard-bitten soldiers probably thought Germanicus weak and bungling. Drusus minor was far tougher with the mutineers in Pannonia, but Tacitus fails to mention this.

On the other hand Germanicus rightly appreciated that the best way of stifling any residual thoughts of mutiny lay in action, and that same autumn launched a punitive expedition into the territory of the Marsi over the Rhine from Vetera, and defeated them, prudently withdrawing, however, before the neighbouring tribes could come to their assistance. Tiberius probably hoped that Germanicus would limit himself to this single action, but Germanicus clearly

had visions of emulating his father and of pushing the Roman frontier east to the Elbe, and pursued a more vigorous and far-reaching campaign in AD 15. The season started both early and well. The Romans advanced north-east and, having recovered the lost *aquila* of *legio XVIIII* on the way, eventually reached the macabre site of the Varian disaster. Moving ceremonies were held in honour of the soldiers who had died under Varus and a funerary mound was raised over the whitened bones and shattered skulls. Germanicus now set off in pursuit of Arminius, the architect of the tragedy, but he made the mistake of penetrating too deep into hostile territory and almost fell into the same trap as had Varus. He extricated himself with difficulty. In full retreat, the exhausted Romans poured over the bridge at Vetera with their honour only just intact.

Another campaign was conducted in AD 16. Germanicus inserted his eight legions by water, sailing along the North Sea coast and up the Weser. After crossing the Weser, Germanicus met the forces of Arminius at a place Tacitus called Idistaviso, and won a first engagement fought on unfavourable ground chosen by the Germans. But Arminius remained at large, and on the return journey disaster struck when the Roman fleet was hit by a storm. Yet Germanicus believed that with one more year he could complete the conquest as far as the Elbe. Tiberius thought otherwise. It was clear to him that further armed intervention east of the Rhine would in fact achieve little, since the defeated foe had the amazing capacity to regroup and to return as vigorous as before. It was time for Germanicus to be recalled. This need not mean that Tiberius was jealous of his adopted son's achievements, as Tacitus strongly hints (*Annales* 2.26.6). From the onset a cool strategist like Tiberius, and an old Germania hand to boot, must have understood that Germanicus' policy was doomed to fail. He rightly appreciated that the conquest of Germania would require a steady policy of pacification with military settlements established in relative proximity, and an extensive network of communications, far from an easy task in a land of primeval forests and swamps.

Anyway, Germanicus returned to Rome a conquering hero. On 26 May AD 17, he celebrated a splendid triumph for his victories over the Cherusci, Chatti and other tribes west of the Elbe (ibid. 2.41.2–4). Tiberius then sent Germanicus to the east in order to deal with a number of serious problems there, in particular the threat of a clash with Parthia. Armenia was without a king, and both Rome and Parthia were anxious to secure a ruler well disposed to them. Whatever Germanicus' deficiencies as a general, he possessed real talents as a diplomat. Thus the emperor's

commission, according to Tacitus (ibid. 2.43.2), granted Germanicus the *imperium* greater than that of any governor in the eastern provinces, that is to say, *imperium pro consule maius*. He proceeded straight to Armenia, where he established as king the Pontic prince Zeno, who adopted the Armenian name Artaxias. He proved to be highly popular

among his new subjects and ruled for 16 years, with the apparent acquiescence of Parthia. Yet his glory in the east was to be short lived. Germanicus fell ill and died in Antioch on 10 October AD 19, at the age of 33. Rumour had it he was poisoned (Suetonius *Tiberius* 54.2, 61.1).

traditional sword-fighting techniques of the Roman Army at Mons Graupius (AD 83), and could even stand up to and beat legionaries as the Batavi rebels did in AD 70 (Tacitus *Annales* 2.16, *Agricola* 36.2, *Historiae* 4.20, 33, 5.16). Indeed, at Mon Graupius the Batavi punched the enemy with their shields and then jabbed them with the sword. Again, we see the *scutum* and *gladius* employed in tandem offensively:

> Accordingly when the Batavi began to exchange blows hand to hand, to strike with the bosses (*umbonis*) of their shields, to stab in the face, and after cutting down the enemy on the level, to push their line uphill, the other *cohortes* [of Tungri], exerting themselves to emulate their charge, proceeded to slaughter the nearest enemies.
> Tacitus *Agricola* 36.2

The essentially similar fighting techniques of the legions and the infantryman of the *auxilia*, that is to come to close-quarters and use both *scutum* and *gladius* offensively, emphasized the degree to which the latter became an essential and very efficient part of the Roman Army. That these tactics were the practice of the period is amply shown on Trajan's Column where at least three scenes of battle depict auxiliaries in action and legionaries in reserve (e.g. scenes xxiv, lxvi, lxxii).

The *alae* would spend their time in peace on manoeuvres and training, while should hostilities break out, they were deployed as a highly mobile strike force, supplemented, if the need arose, by the *cohortes equitatae*. In battle, according to Arrian (*Ektaxis* 1–2, 9, cf. *ILS* 2724 with addenda), the mounted contingents of several *cohortes* were taken from their parent units and massed to form one composite force, roughly equivalent in size to an *ala* (e.g. the horsemen of a *cohors equitata milliaria* amounted in number to almost half an *ala*). It is also clear from reliefs on tombstones depicting *equites cohortales* that they were equipped with the same arms and armour as their more illustrious brothers in the *alae*.

As we well know, when an army deployed for battle it was the infantry who were expected to form up in the centre to fight the main action and deliver the crushing blow. Yet the success of the cavalry in protecting the flanks and defeating their opposite number could decide the outcome, and as such they employed a mix of skirmish and shock tactics and were effectively trained and equipped for both. However, cavalry were not normally expected to charge well-ordered infantry, as the results would have been mutually catastrophic to the opposing front ranks. Besides a horse, especially one being ridden, will not in normal circumstances collide with a solid object if it can stop or go around it. Tacitus (*Historiae* 4.33.2) describes loyal *alae* refusing to charge home on the disciplined ranks of rebel *cohortes*. Cavalry, therefore, would employ typical skirmishing tactics, that is riding up, shooting, wheeling away and then rallying ready to try again. The object of shooting at a steady infantry formation was to weaken it, so that it would unable to stand up to a mounted charge. Outside Ascalon the poorly equipped Jewish infantrymen were quickly reduced by the *lanceae* of the Roman cavalrymen to a state in which they could not stand up to a charge (Josephus *Bellum Iudaicum* 3.13–21).

Reconstruction of a 'cut-down'-style *scutum* in use by Augustus' time, interior view (Caerleon, National Roman Legion Museum). Here we see the reinforcing, which consists of a framework of wooden strips glued or pegged into place. Also visible is the horizontal handgrip. Full-size reconstructions such as this one weigh in the order of 5.5kg. (Fields-Carré Collection)

Similarly, as horses refuse to collide into an oncoming line of horsemen, encounters between opposing cavalry units would have been very fluid, fast-moving affairs. When combats occurred it was because either the two lines had opened their files, allowing them to gallop through each other's formation, or they had halted just before contact, at which point individuals would walk their mounts forward to get within weapon's reach of the enemy. Cavalry combats could sway to and fro as each side beat the enemy, pursued them and were in turn beaten and pursued by fresh enemy troops. Normally the victor was the side that kept a formed, fresh reserve the longest. At Second Cremona, the Flavian cavalry, having routed and pursued several Vitellian *alae*, were themselves put to flight by enemy reserves (Tacitus *Historiae* 3.16.1).

Cavalry was unsuitable to holding ground because of its tendency to advance and retreat rapidly. Thus the tactical principles for its use were: deployment on the wings for flank attacks and encirclement; and deployment in reserve in readiness to counterattack. In brief we cannot do better than to borrow one of those crisp maxims of Napoleon: 'Charges of cavalry are equally useful at the beginning, the middle, and the end of a battle' (*Military Maxims* 50).

Engineering

It is a truism that a soldier's primary *raison d'être* was to wage war, to kill without being killed, and as du Picq sagely remarks, 'man does not go to war in order to fight, but to win' (1946: 5). However, it is important to remember that the Roman soldier was a builder as well as a fighter, and the most common and simplest engineering task carried out by him was building roads. These enabled troops to move more swiftly and supplies to be delivered more efficiently, and were especially important additions to newly acquired territories. The units involved often put up milestones, commemorating the emperor or their legate:

> To the emperor Caesar, son of the divine Nerva, Nerva Traianus Augustus Germanicus Dacicus [i.e. Traianus] *pontifex maximus, tribunicia potestas* XV, *imperator* VI, *consul* V, *pater patriae*, having reduced Arabia to form a province, he opened and paved a new road from the borders of Syria as far as the Red Sea, by Caius Claudius Severus, *legatus Augusti pro praetore*.
> *ILS* 5834

There was one legionary who was not involved in building this new road across Arabia, and that was our friend Iulius Apollinaris. As we know, newly arrived *to legio VI Ferrata fidelis constans*, he had secured for himself a cosy position in headquarters as a 'pen-pusher'.

Marching and practice camps

Josephus says that whenever the Romans entered hostile territory, they would 'first construct their camp' (*Bellum Iudaicum* 3.76). Marching camps, to which Josephus is referring, were overnight halts for armies or units on campaign. These camps, 'constructed more quickly than thought' (ibid. 3.84), provided a simple measure of security for troops camped under canvas.

The kingpin of the whole Flavian system in Caledonia, the fortress at Inchtuthil occupied an area of 21.7ha. Today there is nothing to be seen in the interior of the site, as the internal structures were timber-built. However, this shot, taken from the southern defences, gives an impression of the area covered by a legionary fortress. (Fields-Carré Collection)

Marching camps each had a low earth rampart (*agger*), about five Roman feet (1.48m) in height, topped with some form of timber obstacle. The examples of the square-section wooden stakes (*pila muralia*) for this that have survived are sharpened at both ends, and have a narrower 'waist' in the middle for tying together. They may not, therefore, have been set vertically in the *agger*, as hammering them in would have damaged the sharp ends. Besides, such a palisade would hardly have been very effective as the surviving examples are only five Roman feet (1.48m) in length. It seems more likely that sets of three or four *pila muralia* were lashed together with pliable withies or leather ties at angles and placed on the rampart crown as giant 'caltrops' – what Vegetius (3.8) calls *tribuli*. Although this was never considered a defensive structure, tangling with such an obstacle in an attack would have caused chaos and blunted the impact of an onrush. Whatever the exact employment of the *pilum muralis* – it was probably a very versatile device – each legionary carried one or two *pila muralia*, preferably in oak, as part of his regulation marching order.

Outside the defences was a single V-shaped ditch (*fossa*), usually not more than five Roman feet (1.48m) wide and three Roman feet (89cm) deep, the spoil from which went to form the *agger*. The entrances of marching camps, there were no gateways as such, were of two types. First, those defended by *tituli*, namely short stretches of rampart and ditch set a few metres in front of the gap in the main rampart spanning its width (Hyginus 49). In theory these detached obstacles would break the charge of an enemy. Second, those defended by *claviculae* ('little keys'), namely curved extensions of the rampart (and sometimes its ditch), usually inside the area of the camp (ibid. 55), although external and double *claviculae* are also known from aerial photography. They would force an oblique approach towards the entranceway, usually so that an attacker's sword arm faced the rampart, denying him the protection of his shield.

Within a marching camp the tent-lines were deliberately laid out, each line in its customary space so that every unit knew exactly where to pitch its tents and each man knew his place. Each tent (*papilio*) measured, exclusive of guy-ropes, 10 Roman feet (2.96m) square and housed eight men (*contubernium*) and their equipment (Hyginus 1, cf. Vegetius 2.13). They were made of best quality cattle hide or goatskin with access back and front and enough headroom inside to enable a man to stand up. Made of at least 25 shaped panels, which were sewn together, they could be rolled up into a long sausage-shape and in this form were carried by mule. This shape may have given rise to the nickname *papilio* ('butterfly') as it rolled up like a grub and with its wings probably reminded the soldiers of the insect emerging from the chrysalis. The length of a centurion's tent was twice that of a *papilio*, while those of tribunes and above was taller, box-like structures paved with cut turf.

Two main axes, starting from the entrances, crossed at the centre of the camp; one of them, the *via praetoria*, led from the entrance of the same name to the *porta decumana*, so named because at the time of the manipular legion the tents of the tenth maniples stood nearby; the other, at right angles to it, was the *via principalis*, interrupted at midpoint by the *praetorium*. This was the tent of the general, 'which resembles a temple' (Josephus *Bellum Iudaicum* 3.82). The tribunes' tents ran the length of the *via principalis*, and the surrounding areas were occupied with the soldiers' tents each in its appointed place (ibid. 3.79). Between the rampart and the tent-lines was a wide open area known as the *intervallum*, which ensured all tents were out of range of missiles thrown or shot from outside the camp. More importantly, this space allowed the army to form itself up ready to deploy into battle order. Calculating the number of troops each marching camp would have housed is fraught with difficulties. As a rule of thumb, however, it is usually thought that a full legion could be accommodated under leather in about 30 acres (12ha). The *intervallum* also allowed full access to the defences.

Sex. Iulius Frontinus, onetime governor of Britannia (AD 73–77) and engineer of note, wrote several technical treatises. In one he quotes with approval the maxim of Domitius Corbulo, a commander renowned for his realistic training methods: 'Domitius Corbulo used to say that the pick (*dolabra*) was the weapon with which to beat the enemy' (*Strategemata* 4.7.2). This can only be a reference to the proven ability of the Roman Army to build marching camps for itself. Obviously recruits would have to be instructed in these military techniques, whereas fully trained soldiers would have to be exercised at fairly frequent intervals so as to maintain standards.

Britain easily provides the largest number of practice camps in the empire, the most common size being around 30.5m². Often a kilometre or two away from the site of a fort and close to a Roman road, these sites are where troops trained in constructing marching camps and in particular the most difficult sections of the camps, the corners and gateways. A practice camp has been recognised at Cawthorn, where the legionaries from *VIIII Hispana* based at nearby York (Eburacum), practised not only the art of entrenchment but also the construction of bread-ovens (*clibani*).

Forts and fortresses

Augustus appointed legions and auxiliary units to individual provinces where he perceived a need, either because of inadequate pacification (e.g. Iberia), or because he intended a province to be a platform of aggrandizement (e.g. Germania). Before the Varian disaster, Augustus greatly extended Roman territory in directions that suited him, enhancing his own reputation, acquiring revenue in the form of booty and bringing prestige to the state. During the winter months, the troops were scattered and stationed in winter quarters (*castra hiberna*), before being assembled in camps (*castra aestiva*) for summer campaigns (e.g. Tacitus *Historiae* 3.46.2, *Annales* 1.16.2, 30.3). Of course the latter installations would also include the camps built at the end of every day during campaigns. Equally, winter quarters were not permanent – the Augustan ones on the Rhine show evidence of frequent modifications – and in more urbanized provinces, such as Syria, the troops could be billeted in towns and cities.

As noted, when an army was on campaign it constructed marching camps to provide security at night, but once an area was conquered it laid down a network of smaller turf and timber forts roughly a day's march apart. Under Claudius, when a belated recognition came that the Roman Army was no longer poised to continue the Augustan expansion of the empire, these winter quarters and

The multiplication of defensive ditches (five in all) on the north and east sides of Ardoch fort is the result of successive reductions in its size and not of anxiety over its security. Initially the Flavian fort had an area of some 3.5ha, but that of the Antonine period had been reduced to about 2.3ha. (Fields-Carré Collection)

wayside forts became permanent. Britannia's garrison, for instance, fluctuated between three and four legions during the 1st century AD, depending on the demands of other provinces, but from the late 80s AD the number remained at three, though not always the same three, with their permanent camps, or what are conveniently labelled legionary fortresses, at Isca Silurum (Caerleon), Deva (Chester) and Eburacum (York). Likewise, some auxiliary units were beginning to be stationed in separate forts; the earliest known auxiliary fort is that at Valkenburg in southern Holland, constructed in AD 40 or thereabouts.

It should be emphasized that there is no such thing as a typical Roman fortress or fort. The layout of a fortress, for instance, was standardized, but a close examination of fortress layouts shows that there were considerable differences in detail between individual fortress plans, and between the same types of building at different sites. All the same, their plan and design preserved the main defensive features of the marching camp from which they had evolved. The shallow ditch and palisade of the latter were, however, replaced by more substantial earthworks in permanent camps, often with two or more V-shaped ditches and an earth or turf rampart surmounted by a timber parapet. The four gateways were retained, but towers now defended them, and further towers were added at the four angles and at intervals between.

Roman commanders favoured large concentrations of soldiers and generally, prior to Domitianus, fortresses were permanent camps accommodating two legions. This was a concentration of some 10,000 legionaries in a single spot, and we find two such spots on the Rhine where in AD 69 Vetera (Xanten-Birten) was garrisoned by *V Alaudae* and *XV Primigenia*, and Mogontiacum (Mainz) by *IIII Macedonica* and *XXII Primigenia*.

However, as the result of the rebellion in AD 89 of L. Antonius Saturninus, governor of Germania Superior, who induced the two legions (*XIIII Gemina Martia Victrix* and *XXI Rapax*) based at Moguntiacum to support his cause, Domitianus issued a regulation forbidding in future more than one legion to occupy the same

Reconstruction of a timber gateway with a section of earth and turf rampart topped with a spilt-timber palisade, Chesterholm-Vindolanda. This represents the usual defences of a military installation of our period, be it fortress or fort. Note the access to the wall-walk is via a fixed wooden stairway and that to the tower via a ladder. (Fields-Carré Collection)

camp (Suetonius *Domitianus* 7.4). Thus the two legions at Moguntiacum were separated, and the fortress cut to one legion (*XIIII Gemina Martia Victrix*), and in general fortresses were reduced in size (*c.*20–25ha) to house a single legion. The one exception to Domitianus' regulation was Egypt, where the two legions that formed its garrison (*III Cyrenaica* and *XXII Deiotariana*) were concentrated in one camp at Nikopolis just outside Alexandria, continuing to do so till at least AD 119 when one was transferred to allow the reinforcement of the garrison of troublesome Iudaea.

As the army began to adopt a primarily defensive role and surveillance of the frontier itself began to assume greater importance, the auxiliary units were gradually spaced out, garrisoning forts between and beyond the legionary fortresses. Indeed, the framework of Roman occupation and control was firmly based on the fort (c. one to five hectares), a permanent camp accommodating an auxiliary unit. The layout of the auxiliary fort was essentially a miniature of the legionary fortress plan. During our period a fort was protected by an earth rampart – revetted with either timber or turf and founded upon a corduroy of logs or a stone base – surmounted by a spilt-timber breastwork or woven wattle-work hurdles and fronted by one or more V-shaped ditches. The rampart was pierced by four gateways, each with a timber tower above the gate passage itself or towers to either side. Further towers, set within the body of the rampart, stood at the angles as well as being spaced at regular intervals around the perimeter.

Tacitus rightly calls the fort the 'soldiers' hearth and home' (*Historiae* 2.80.4), the objective being to provide a permanent and tolerably comfortable quarter for its garrison. As such, it was hardly inferior in its facilities to the fortress of the legions. It must also be secure from the possibility of surprise attack. Yet a fort was not designed as an impregnable stronghold; on the contrary it was a jumping-off point, a base for wide-ranging activities. In wartime the enemy was engaged at close-quarters in the field, while at other times the garrison would have patrolled well beyond the frontier either to support allied tribes or to conduct punitive campaigns.

Siegeworks

Siege warfare was a haphazard affair at the best of times and not undertaken lightly. However, if a Roman commander chose to conduct a siege, he had three modes of action at his disposal: well-trained troops, machines and siegeworks.

A siege normally followed a recognized pattern of events. The first and obvious phase was to impose a blockade, with the aim of starving the besieged into submission. The second phase provided a natural corollary to this: a line of entrenchments, known as a contravallation, was dug and erected around the objective, out of range of missile weapons, mechanical or manpowered, with the dual purpose of denying access to or issue from the objective and of providing to the besiegers shelter from surprise attack from within. In its simplest form the contravallation was no more than an *agger*, though more often than not the earth rampart was reinforced by a ditch and palisade. The third phase of a siege comprised the development of a further line of entrenchments, known as a circumvallation, which faced away from the objective and protected the rear of the besiegers from possible attack from without. Of course this was an optional expedient, the Romans besieging Masada (AD 73–74) opting to encircle the target only with a contravallation.

Naturally, the circuit wall itself was the chief obstacle to the besieger. A breach could be achieved by attacking it under cover of a 'tortoise' (*testudo*) with a battering ram (*aries*), or by digging a mine into which the wall would collapse, or else digging a tunnel underneath the wall. As well as going through or under the wall, it was also possible to go over it by employing a siege tower suitably fitted with a boarding-bridge.

Jotapata (Mizpe Yodefat) in Galilee was 'perched on a precipice, cut off on three sides by ravines of such extraordinary depth' (Josephus *Bellum Iudaicum* 3.158). The only access was from the north, where a wall had been built to prevent such a thing, and it was here that Vespasianus pitched his camp sometime early in AD 67. Several days followed during which the Jewish rebels made a number of sorties against the Romans. Vespasianus now decided to prosecute the siege with vigour, throwing up a ramp of earth and timber against the wall. Though the soldiers forming the work-parties were protected by sheds (*vineae*), timber and wickerwork structures sheeted in fire-resistant rawhides, they were greatly impeded by the missiles hurled at them by the defenders.

Vespasianus now set 160 two-armed torsion machines (*ballistae*), of various calibres and firing either arrows or stones, to work to dislodge the enemy from the wall. The Jews retaliated by making swift sallies 'guerrilla-fashion' and demolishing the sheds. However, the work on the siege ramp continued, and Josephus, the rebel leader, decided to build the wall higher at this point, accomplishing this by having a screen of rawhides of newly slaughtered oxen strung along the top of the wall to protect the workers. The hides broke the impact of the incoming missiles, and being moist, they quenched those of a fiery nature (ibid. 3.165–75).

During the Jewish War, when Jotapata fell Josephus fled to a cave with a band of followers. Here he was discovered after all but one of his men had dispatched each other rather than surrender. Dragged before Vespasianus, the future historian, grovelling, 'prophesied' his elevation to the purple. Mid-16th century Flemish tapestry (Marsala, Museo delgi Arazzi, Tapestry 5) showing Vespasianus releasing Josephus. (Fields-Carré Collection)

The besieged had plenty of grain but little water, so Josephus caused water to be rationed at an early stage. The besiegers got wind of this and took heart, believing the siege almost over. But the people of Jotapata confounded them by washing out their clothes in their precious water. These being hung out to dry on the battlements, the walls soon ran with water. The Romans thought they must have some secret source of supply.

Josephus now decided to quit Jotapata, believing it would draw the Romans away, but the people pleaded with him not to leave them, and so he stayed and organized many sorties. The Romans counteracted with their artillery, which was now augmented with Syrian slingers and Arab bowmen, but all this made the Jews even more determined to resist.

T. Flavius Vespasianus (d. AD 79)
Some 90 years after Actium, the Iulio-Claudian dynasty had come to a tragic and untimely end. In the pithy observation of Tacitus, Nero's death by his own shaky hand had 'let out the secret that an emperor could be made elsewhere than at Rome' (*Historiae* 1.4.1). Vespasianus, a senator of obscure Italian origin, would come out of the civil war of AD 68–69 as the founder of a new dynasty.

Nero had entrusted Vespasianus with the command in Iudaea (three legions, plus four more in Syria) because he was 'an energetic commander, who could be trusted not to abuse his plenary powers ... nothing, it seemed, need be feared from a man of such modest antecedents' (Suetonius *Vespasianus* 4.5). Significantly, the 'base-born' Vespasianus, along with his son Titus, would acquire from the bitter Jewish war a reputation for sharing the toils of the army and identifying themselves with the common soldier. Vespasianus was a natural soldier: he led the column-of-march in person, selected camp sites, pursued the enemy day and night, and would even venture into the battle line if necessary, thus committing himself to the trial of combat; he ate whatever rations were available and in dress and appearance was much the same as an ordinary ranker (Tacitus *Historiae* 2.5.1).

Vespasianus, who obviously came across as more a soldier than a politician, built up an excellent rapport with his men. The imperial pretence was that power came from the Roman people by voluntary grant, whereas in reality it was either inherited (as in the case of Tiberius) or seized (as in the case of Vespasianus). Likewise, the fairytale fiction that the army was the army of the Roman people was preserved. Tiberius might proclaim 'the legions are not mine but the state's' (Cassius Dio 57.2.3), but in truth the emperor commanded what was virtually his own private army. This reminds us of the theory and practice in the ex-Soviet Union. As Henry Kissinger once majestically commented:

> No Communist state has solved the problem of regular succession. Every leader dies in office, or is replaced by coup-like procedures. Honorific retirement is rare and non-existent for the supreme leader. No Soviet leader's reputation, except Lenin's, has survived his death. In every Communist state a leadership group seize power, grow old together, and are eventually replaced by successors whose ability to reach the pinnacle depends on their skill in masking their ambitions ... they know that they will probably be denied by their successors the accolade of history, which is the incentive of most statesmen. Kissinger, H.A., 1979, *The White House Years*, London: Weidenfeld & Nicolson, 113.

Beside Kissinger's last point we can place a comment by Cassius Dio, namely that 'no injunction can have any weight against the ingratitude or the might of one's successors' (59.1.3).

Vespasianus was an able military commander and politician. He was well liked by Claudius, being granted *triumphalia* for his part in the invasion of Britannia, but ran afoul of Nero, who sent him to Iudaea to handle the Jewish revolt. Vespasianus quickly succeeded in quelling the violence and was set to invest Jerusalem when Nero played his last scene.

At first, Vespasianus supported Galba, whom the Senate had confirmed as emperor, and then Otho. But the ensuing civil war and rapid departures of the two emperors made Vespasianus realize he could make a play for the purple. When legions under the control of Vespasianus' political allies declared him emperor, the Senate confirmed it. This brought an end to the civil war, and in recognition of this accomplishment Vespasianus built a new temple of peace, the Templum Pacis. Thus he emphasized the stability of Roman power, with the empire once again set on the firmest foundations both politically and militarily.

The only charge held against Vespasianus was his avarice (Tacitus *Historiae* 2.5.2, Suetonius *Vespasianus* 16.1). As emperor he was a conscientious, firm and responsible leader – exactly what the empire needed. He immediately attended to the matter of his succession and declared in the Senate that either his sons would succeed him or no one would. He reorganized the army, filled the coffers that Nero and the civil war had depleted, began building the Flavian Amphitheatre, better known to history as the Colosseum, and taught his son Titus about governing so that the Flavian dynasty would thrive after his death. His sense of humour showed through when on his deathbed, dying of fever, he is reported to have uttered the words, 'Oh, I think I'm becoming a god' (Suetonius *Vespasianus* 23).

Vespasianus now brought up a battering ram, and at the very first strike the wall was shaken 'and piercing shrieks were raised by those within, as if the town had been captured already' (ibid. 3.220). Josephus tried to defeat the ram by ordering sacks to be filled with chaff and lowering them down over the wall so that they would weaken its blows. Each time the Romans moved their ram to a new spot, so the defenders did likewise with their bales of chaff (ibid. 3.223). In the end the Romans managed to cut the bales from off the ropes and so continued their battering of the wall. Three parties of the rebels then rushed out of the gates and, armed with dry wood mixed with bitumen and pitch, made a bonfire of the ram. While this was going on, a Jew, renowned for his might, cast a huge stone down from the wall and on to the ram and broke off its iron head. Before the Romans could effectively respond, the Jews torched many of the other machines, but this did not prevent the besiegers from erecting the ram again and continuing their battering of the wall (ibid. 3.227–28).

It was about now that Vespasianus was wounded in the foot by an arrow, which so incensed his soldiers that they renewed their attack on the city regardless. Incidentally, Tacitus describes the future emperor as 'a worthy successor to the commanders of old' (*Historiae* 2.5.1), that is to say, leading from the front and setting an example to his 'fellow soldiers' (*commilitones*). Anyway, in the meantime the defenders still clung stubbornly to Jotapata's crumbling battlements, and Josephus recounts how one of the men standing close to him was decapitated and his head flung hundreds of metres from the body. Even more shocking was the fate of a pregnant woman obviously caught up willy-nilly in the horrors of the siege. She was shattered by an incoming stone just as she stepped out of her house at sun-up, and the unborn child was flung some distance away (*Bellum Iudaicum* 3.245–46).

That same daybreak, having finally breached the wall, the Romans prepared for the final assault, but were forestalled by the rebels charging out to meet them. While a furious fight ensued the Romans attempted to scale the unbreached part of the wall, but this move was checked by the stratagem of scalding oil, the first recorded use of this weapon. The defenders then quickly resorted to a second ruse: they poured boiled fenugreek (*Faenum Graecum*, 'Greek hay') upon the boards which the Romans were using in their attempt to scale the wall, thus making them so slippery as to be unusable (ibid. 3.275–78).

Undaunted by this setback, Vespasianus ordered his men to raise the siege-mounds higher and to erect three towers on them. Each 50 Roman feet (14.8m) high and encased in iron on all four sides, the towers housed *ballistae* and their operators, while from their lofty tops javelineers, slingers and archers were able to pour missiles down on the heads of the now-unprotected defenders on the wall.

By the 47th day of the siege a deserter went to Vespasianus and informed him of the pitiful state of the defenders. He also told of how the Jews, all-in from the constant fighting and vigilance, usually slept during the last watch of the night. And so at the appointed hour a Roman assault party noiselessly made their way silently to the wall, cut the throats of the watch and snuck into the sleeping town. The Jews were taken by surprise, more so as a thick swirling mist confounded their efforts to organize an effective resistance. In all about 40,000 were slain at the siege of Jotapata, with 1,200 women and children auctioned off as slaves. Vespasianus' final order was for the town to be razed to the ground.

After Actium

There is always a certain degree of ambiguity about what exactly Augustus was trying achieve by his constitutional settlements of 27 and 23 BC. Suetonius (*Divus Augustus* 28.2) cites one of his edicts of 27 BC, which strongly suggests Augustus saw himself as a founder of a new constitutional system. Whatever, Augustus' achievements were considerable. He established a system of administration effective not only in Rome and Italy but also in the provinces. He held the government firmly on the basis of the authority of a popular tribune (*tribunicia potestas*), a proconsular power (*imperium pro consule*) superior (*maius*) to any individual senatorial proconsul, granted for life and valid even within the city of Rome (where normally *imperium pro consule* lapsed), and control of the provinces where, with three exceptions, the legions were stationed. Outwardly, his administration adhered broadly to a republican framework. He still used the Senate as a legislative and judicial body, and instituted six-monthly consultative committees, using a small number of leading senators as a cabinet (*consilium principis*) to formulate proposals that would then be put before the Senate as a whole. Yet in truth it was a new political order dressed up as a restoration, an autocracy with republican trimmings. Besides, as Fergus Millar (1992: 6) so aptly puts it, 'the emperor was what the emperor did'.

The legions had been the source of Augustus' power. However, serious mutinies broke out in Pannonia and Germania in AD 14 partly because the legionaries were worried about their conditions of service after the death of Augustus, so closely had he become associated with their emoluments. But there was obviously significant discontent with low rates of pay, especially in contrast to the praetorians, long service and unsuitable land allocations. Here Tacitus takes up the story:

> Finally Percennius had acquired a team of helpers ready for mutiny. Then he made something like a public speech. 'Why', he asked, 'obey, like slaves, a few commanders of centuries, fewer still of cohorts? You will never be brave enough to demand better conditions if you are not prepared to

In order to control what was a vast territory, which theoretically encompassed all Germania east of the Rhine and up to the Elbe, Varus had five legions: three, *XVII, XVIII* and *XVIIII*, with him in the north stationed at Vetera (Xanten-Birten), and two more, *I* (later *I Germanica*) and *V Alaudae*, under a legate, his nephew L. Asprenas, in the south stationed at Mogontiacum (Mainz). With the three legions under his personal command, Varus also had six *cohortes* and three *alae* of *auxilia*.

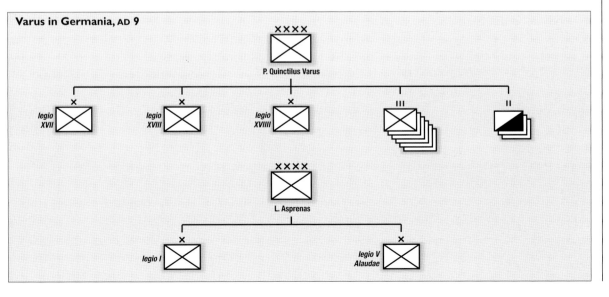

Varus in Germania, AD 9

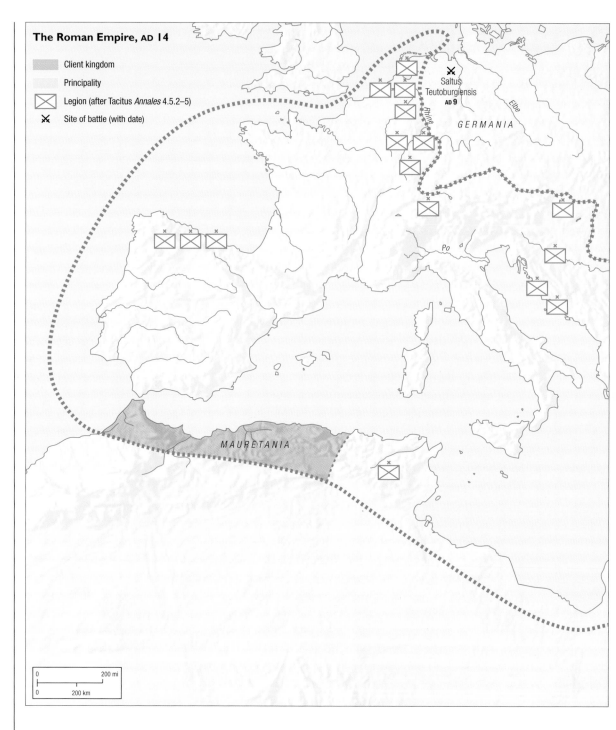

The Roman Empire, AD 14

Client kingdom

Principality

Legion (after Tacitus *Annales* 4.5.2–5)

Site of battle (with date)

Saltus Teutoburgiensis AD 9

GERMANIA

Elbe

Rhine

Po

MAURETANIA

0   200 mi

0   200 km

Tranquillity for Italy, peace in the provinces and the security of empire: these are listed by Caesar (*Bellum civile* 3.57.4) as the basic achievements for a statesman. The prime means of attaining them was the legions. When a standing army was fully recognized towards the middle of Augustus' reign, it was composed of 28 legions, half of which were stationed in the provinces of the northern frontiers from Gaul to Macedonia. This number was reduced to 25 after the Varian disaster of AD 9, when three legions were lost in Germania. At the legion's paper strength this meant that some 125,000 Roman citizens were under arms. These were supported by an equal number of auxiliaries.

On Augustus' death Rome controlled, either directly or through subservient client kingdoms, most of the territories round the Mediterranean basin upon which its security depended. Tacitus, on Tiberius' first debate in the Senate as the new emperor, has this to say: 'A note book was produced, containing the details of the matters concerning the state, the extent of citizens and allies under arms, the size of the fleets, of kingdoms, provinces, taxes and revenues, necessary expenses and donations. All this Augustus had

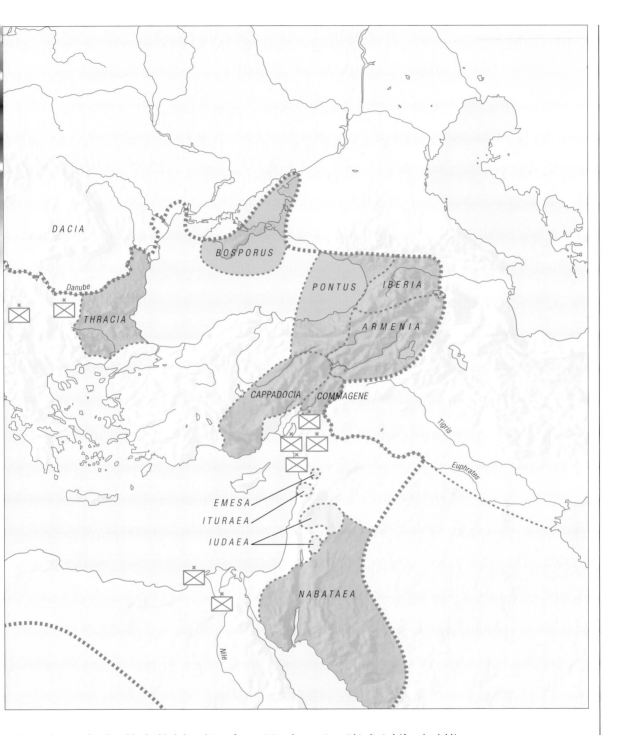

written in his own hand, and had added the advice of restraining the empire within limits' (*Annales* 1.11).

Whether or not this document was genuine or, for that matter, ever existed, Tiberius, although he had been one of the most experienced of the Augustan commanders, was to follow the so-called Augustan mandate to the letter. With years of fighting on the Rhine and the Danube, Tiberius felt that the costs involved in conquering and pacifying new territories, even further from the Mediterranean, outweighed the possible benefits.

Yet, as we would expect in a militaristic society, there was a consciousness among Roman commanders of a 'heroic past' that they felt drawn to emulate. Tacitus records the verbal outburst of Domitius Corbulo, the serving governor of Germania Inferior and one of the most distinguished commanders of our period, when instructed by Claudius in AD 47 to stop further aggression against the Chauci: 'Earlier Roman commanders were fortunate!' (ibid. 11.21.3).

petition – or even threaten – an emperor who is new and still faltering [i.e. Tiberius]. Inactivity has done quite enough harm in all these years. Old men, mutilated by wounds, are serving their 30th year or 40th year. And even after your official discharge your service is not finished; for you stay on with the colours as a reserve (*sue vexillo*), still under canvas – the same drudgery under another name! And if you manage to survive all these hazards, even then you are dragged off to a remote country and 'settled' in some waterlogged swamp or uncultivated mountainside. Truly the army is aharsh, unrewarding profession! Body and soul are reckoned at ten *asses* a day – and with this you have to find clothes, weapons, tents, and bribes for brutal centurions if you want to avoid chores.

Tacitus *Annales* 1.17

Percennius, a common soldier, was the ringleader of the mutineers in Pannonia, then garrisoned by three legions (*VIII Augusta*, *VIIII Hispana* and *XV Apollinaris*) based in a camp near Emona (Ljubljana). Once the mutiny was crushed he was to be hunted down and executed for his troubles.

These mutinies clearly showed the danger of having too many legions (there were four involved in the Germania mutiny) in the same camp. Also living in tents, even during the summer months, on the Rhine and Danube frontiers must have been miserable to say the least. The bleakness of life under canvas is the subject of a telling passage of Tertullian: 'No soldier comes with frolics to battle nor does he go to the front from his bedroom but from tents that are light and small, where there is every kind of hardship, inconvenience, and discomfort' (*ad Martyras* 3).

In the time of Augustus the annual rate of pay for a legionary was 225 *denarii*, Percennius' 'ten asses a day' (Tacitus *Annales* 1.17.6). But Percennius' complaint was all in vain, the basic rate remaining so until Domitianus, who increased the pay by one third, that is, to 300 *denarii* a year (Suetonius *Domitianus* 7.35, 12.1). Wages were paid in three annual instalments (Cassius Dio 67.3.5), the first payment being made on the occasion of the annual New Year parade when the troops renewed their oath to the emperor. Official deductions were made for food and fodder (for the mule belonging to the *contubernium*). In addition, each soldier had to pay for his own clothing, equipment and weapons (e.g. Campbell 24, 25), but these items were purchased back by the army from the soldier or his heir when he retired or died. These were the official charges. As we know, Tacitus

Stationed in Germania Inferior, under A. Caecina Severus, there were four legions: two, *I Germanica* and *XX* (later *XX Valeria Victrix*), at Oppidum Ubiorum (Köln), and two more, *V Alaudae* and *XXI Rapax*, at Vetera (Xanten-Birten). Stationed in Germania Superior, under C. Silius (*cos.* AD 13), there were four legions: three, *XIIII Gemina* (later *XIIII Gemina Martia Victrix*), *XVI Gallica* and *II Augusta*, at Mogontiacum (Mainz), with another one, *XIII Gemina*, to the south at Vindonissa (Windisch). As befitting a prince, two cohorts of praetorians were acting as Germanicus' bodyguard.

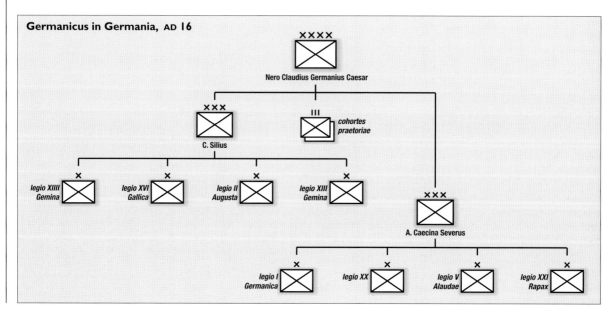

Germanicus in Germania, AD 16

records that one of the complaints of the mutineers was that they had to pay sweeteners to venal centurions in order to gain exemption from fatigues. Another complaint was that time-expired soldiers were being fobbed off with grants of land in lieu of the gratuity of 3,000 *denarii*, and these plots tended to be either waterlogged or rock-strewn.

There was also a serious guerrilla war in Africa started by the Numidian Tacfarinas, a deserter from the ranks of the *auxilia*. Equipping and organizing his native army along Roman lines (Tacitus *Annales* 2.52.3), he managed to keep the Romans busy for nigh-on eight years (AD 17–24). Eventually, through a system of forts and the deployment of mobile columns specially trained for desert conditions, Tacfarinas and his guerrillas were constantly engaged and thus worn down. As the legions and auxiliary units became more static, and widely spaced, the problem of responding to particular threats became more acute. For this reason *VIIII Hispana* was transferred from Pannonia to Africa for four years to assist *III Augusta* in quelling the native revolt (ibid. 3.9.1, 4.23.2).

The establishment of the Principate by Augustus had banished war to the social and geographical periphery. Professional soldiers now fought wars, and these normally took place on distant frontiers. But with the death of Nero, the last of Augustus' bloodline, the empire was plunged into a civil war as vicious as any of those that had dogged the final decades of the Republic. A century of internal peace and stability would be shattered as armies were assembled and pitted against each other by four emperors in rapid succession.

Ser. Sulpicius Galba (b. 3 BC) had a successful military career and was a close friend of Claudius, who had selected him as governor of Africa. He was now governor of Hispania Tarraconensis, the largest of the three Iberian provinces. Nero had just returned from his artistic tour of Greece, when in March AD 68 news reached him that C. Iulius Vindex, governor of Gallia Lugdunensis and himself an Aquitani chieftain, had risen up in rebellion. This did not do Vindex much good; in May his inexperienced troops were cut to pieces by the Rhine legions. The victorious soldiers wanted to proclaim their commander Verginius Rufus emperor, but he sensibly declined the offer. Meanwhile in Iberia, the soldiers of *VI Victrix* declared their man emperor. Galba accepted, and eventually the Senate (and the praetorians) confirmed it. The Sulpicii Galbae had been prominent in senatorial politics for more than two centuries and Galba's claim to the imperial purple was at least in part based on his distinguished republican aristocratic ancestry.

By the time Galba reached Rome Nero had breathed his last. For the moment, he refused the title of emperor, but it is clear that the Principate was his goal. To this end, he organized a *concilium* of advisors in order to make it known that any decisions were not made by him alone but only after consultation with a group. The arrangement was meant to recall the healthy relationship between Augustus and the Senate. Even more revealing of his imperial ambitions were legends like LIBERTAS RESTITUTA ('Liberty Restored') and SALUS GENERIS HUMANI ('Salvation of Mankind'), preserved on the coins he issued as emperor, and it is interesting to note that Vindex, before he went down, had urged Galba to 'make himself the liberator and leader of humanity' (Suetonius *Galba* 9.2). Such evidence has brought into question the traditional assessment of Galba as nothing more than an

Marble bust of Livia (d. AD 29), dated to the 1st century AD (Selçuk, Arkeoloji Müzesi). Tacitus portrays Livia as a very powerful influence on both Augustus and Tiberius, while Phaedrus, a satirist who flourished under Tiberius, published the fable of the she-goats' beards. It seems Livia wore the trousers in the imperial house. (Fields-Carré Collection)

Coin depicting the head of Nero Claudius Drusus. Brother of Tiberius and father of Germanicus, Drusus campaigned extensively in Germania and managed to reach the Elbe. It is said he spent much time chasing various Germanic chieftains on the battlefield in the hope of overcoming them in mortal combat. (Ancient Art and Architecture)

In Britannia at the time there were four legions. Of these, *VIIII Hispana* was to be too badly mauled in an ambush to play any further part in the campaign, while *II Augusta*, then in the south-west of the province, failed to join Suetonius Paulinus. Thus the governor was left with only those troops under his immediate command, namely *XIIII Gemina* (soon *XIIII Gemina Martia Victrix*) and a part of *XX Valeria* (soon *XX Valeria Victrix*) plus some auxiliary units.

ineffectual representative of a bygone age in favour of a more balanced portrait of a traditional constitutionalist eager to publicize the virtues of an Augustan-style Principate.

Although not a bad administrator, Galba was lecherous and cruel, and quickly managed to alienate everyone including the military; when asked to approve a pay increase for the army he took the line of high principle and notoriously declared, 'I pick my soldiers, I do not buy them' (Tacitus *Historiae*

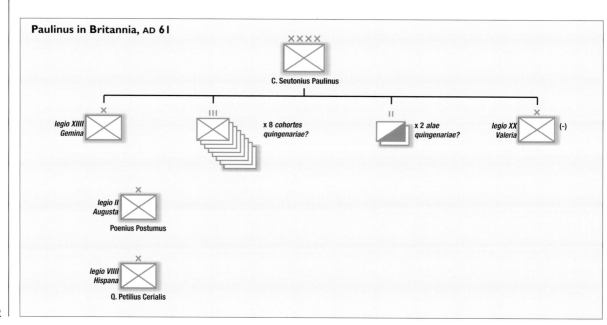

Paulinus in Britannia, AD 61

XXXX

C. Seutonius Paulinus

legio XIIII Gemina

x 8 cohortes quingenariae?

x 2 alae quingenariae?

legio XX Valeria (-)

legio II Augusta

Poenius Postumus

legio VIIII Hispana

Q. Petilius Cerialis

Vespasianus, who owed a great deal to the navy for opening the seaways to Italy during his bid for power, settled veterans from the Ravenna and Misene fleets at Paestum. Dated to the late 1st century AD, this is the tombstone of C. Valerius Naso, a marine in the *centuria* of Secundus. He died aged 40 after 23 years' service. (Fields-Carré Collection)

1.5.3). On 2 January AD 69 the end was already in sight. The legions in Germania Superior (*IIII Macedonica*, *XXI Rapax* and *XXII Primigenia*) refused to recognize him as their commander-in-chief and proclaimed Aulus Vitellius, governor of next-door Germania Inferior, emperor. A fortnight later, in broad daylight, Galba was butchered in the Forum by his own praetorians, seduced by Otho.

M. Salvius Otho was one of Nero's closest friends and confidants, making him a powerful figure. However, Otho's imperial favour wavered when Nero took a strong liking to his wife, the ambitious Poppaea Sabina, and he was 'banished' to Lusitania to serve as its governor. Out of revenge (and in hopes of great personal gains) Otho assisted Galba in becoming emperor. When the elderly Galba, whose two sons had both died at a young age, adopted a certain L. Calpurnius Piso Frugi Licinianus, a long-named but little-known scion of old Roman nobility, as his son and successor, a firm friend was turned into a mortal enemy (Tacitus *Historiae* 1.13). Having turned to the praetorians, who happily proclaimed him emperor, Otho had them remove Galba, along with Piso, while the Senate hastened to recognize him.

Fortune did not favour Otho, however, because he was immediately faced with Vitellius' army, which was marching on Italy. Otho proposed a system of joint rule and was even willing to marry Vitellius' daughter, but the tide could not be turned. For Otho there was no other solution but to face the opposing army. On 14 March he left Rome and made camp in Bedriacum (Tornato), just north of the Padus (Po), some 30km from Cremona. On 14 April the decisive confrontation took place, in a neighbourhood thick with vineyards somewhere between Bedriacum and Cremona. Badly outnumbered by that of Vitellius, Otho's army was quickly defeated; deserted, he put his affairs in order and committed suicide, apparently to avoid further bloodshed.

To be sure, Otho remains an enigma – part Neronian wastrel and part conscientious commander willing to give his life for the good of the state. Our sources are at a loss to explain the paradox. Perhaps he saw it was safer to appear a profligate in Nero's court. In the final analysis, Otho proved to be an organized and efficient general, who appealed more to the soldier than to the civilian. He also seems to have been a capable governor, with administrative talents that recalled those of his brilliant father. Nevertheless, his violent overthrow of Galba, the lingering doubts that it raised about his character and

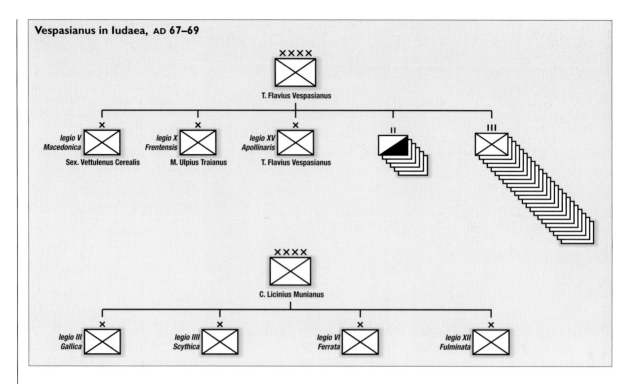

Vespasianus in Iudaea, AD 67–69

When a renewed bout of fighting against Parthia flared up in Nero's reign, and a strong military presence was politically as well as militarily desirable in the east, two legions, *IIII Scythica* and *V Macedonica*, were moved there from Moesia, and one other, *XV Apollinaris*, from Pannonia. All three legions would remain in the east throughout the Jewish revolt, with *XV Apollinaris* never returning but ending up as the new garrison of Cappadocia in AD 72.

So when Vespasianus took up the Iudaean command in the winter of AD 67, his army consisted of three legions, *V Macedonica*, *X Fretensis* and *XV Apollinaris*. Josephus tells us that these were supported by 23 *cohortes*, of which ten were *peditatae milliariae* and the rest *equitatae quingenariae*, and six *alae*. Meanwhile, there were four other legions, *III Gallica*, *IIII Scythica*, *VI Ferrata* and *XII Fulminata*, in next-door Syria with the governor C. Licinius Mucianus. In AD 68 *III Gallica* would be transferred from Syria to Moesia.

The legate of *XV Apollinaris* was none other than Vespasianus' eldest son, Titus. This unit had seen a little service at the end of Domitius Corbulo's Parthian campaign but lacked the experience of the other legions. At 27 years of age Titus was younger than most legionary legates and his appointment reflects the tradition of senators relying on family members to serve as their senior subordinates. Another of Vespasianus' subordinates was M. Ulpius Traianus, the legate of *X Fretensis*. He was, of course, the father and namesake of the future emperor, Traianus.

his unsuccessful offensive against Vitellius are all vivid reminders of the turbulence that plagued the Roman world between the reigns of Nero and Vespasianus. Regrettably, the scenario would play itself out one more time before peace and stability returned to the empire.

Vitellius was well liked by Caligula, Claudius and Nero. As governor of Germania Superior he governed reasonably well, but his many vices usually got the best of him. As noted, when Galba became emperor the Rhine legions refused to pledge allegiance to him, declaring their own man the emperor. This was partially out of hatred for the parsimonious Galba, and partially out of fondness for the pleasure-seeking Vitellius. Upon learning of Galba's death, Vitellius gathered up two of the Rhine legions, along with *vexillationes* from the other five, and sent them on to Rome. He was certainly no soldier, for he stayed put on the Rhine while his army did his dirty work near the Padus. When the hapless Otho committed suicide, the hedonistic Vitellius was left as sole emperor. After a tour of the battlefield near Cremona, he entered Rome in the middle of July and proclaimed himself consul for life. Contrary to expectations he showed himself to be moderate. However, he soon received word that the legions of the east had declared themselves in favour of that successful and popular general, Vespasianus, and before long the Danube legions followed suit.

Titus (now dead and deified) rides in his triumph 'over the Jews', Arch of Titus, Rome. The triumph, with its parade of spoils, captives, soldiers, divine images and pictorial scenes of the war, was the most direct expression of an emperor's personal military glory. It was also attractive since it retailed many of the respected traditions of the Republic. (Fields-Carré Collection)

It was the six Danube legions that put an end to Vitellius' reign. Under the dynamic leadership of Antonius Primus, legate of Galba's newly formed *VII Hispana*, which was currently bearing the moniker *Galbiana* and serving in Pannonia (Tacitus *Historiae* 2.86.1, cf. 3.7.1, 21.2), the Flavian legions made a rapid descent on Italy, and on the night of 24/25 October, practically at the same spot outside Cremona where Vitellius' army had been so successful before, there was a decisive battle. The Vitellians were soundly beaten. For four days the victorious Flavians wreaked bloody havoc on Cremona. Meantime, Vitellius occupied the Apennine passes in an attempt to halt the advance, but his men defected in droves. Vitellius had no choice but to retreat to Rome. On 20 December Antonius Primus reached the gates of the city and fought his way in. His soldiers found Vitellius, tortured him to death in public and then threw his corpse into the Tiber, thus ending the civil war and beginning the Flavian rule. On the whole, it seems the very bad portrayal of him in the sources derives from the inherent hostility of the Flavian writers and the manner of his demise, which was by no means as edifying as Otho's.

And so Vitellius has not escaped the hostility of his biographers. While he may well have been gluttonous, his depiction as indolent, cruel and extravagant is based almost entirely on the propaganda of his enemies. Hence Tacitus' description of Vitellius' triumphal entry into Rome:

> In front of the eagles marched the camp prefects, tribunes and front-ranker centurions (*primi ordines*), all dressed in white. The other officers each flanked their own centuries, resplendent in their weapons and decorations. As for the soldiers, they glistened with their *phalerae* and torques. It was an awesome sight, an army worthy of an emperor other than Vitellius.
> Tacitus *Historiae* 2.89.3

On the other hand, whatever moderating tendencies he did show were overshadowed by his clear lack of military expertise, a deficiency that forced him to rely in critical situations on largely ineffective lieutenants. As a result he was no match for his Flavian successors, and his humiliating demise was perfectly in keeping with the overall fiasco of his fleeting reign.

Agricola in Caledonia, AD 82–83

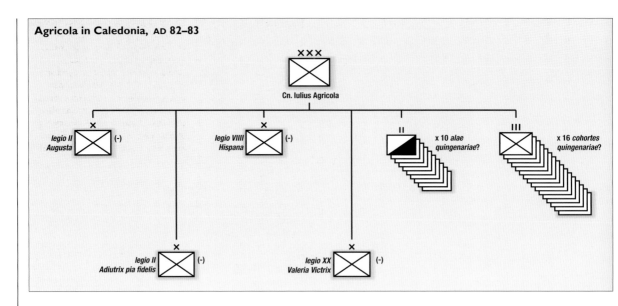

For his two seasons north of the Bodotria (Forth), Agricola had mustered *vexillationes* from the four legions, *II Adiutrix pia fidelis*, *II Augusta*, *VIIII Hispana* and *XX Valeria Victrix*, of Britannia. These were supported by some 8,000 auxiliary infantry and 5,000 auxiliary cavalry. Of the *auxilia*, we know of four *cohortes* of Batavi, two *cohortes* of Tungri and an unspecified number of Britons recruited from the tribes in the south. If the *auxilia* were organized as *quingenaria* units, then Agricola would have had some 16 *cohortes* and ten *alae* all told.

Cn. Iulius Agricola, (AD 40–93)

Born in the colony of Forum Iulii (Fréjus) in Gallia Narbonensis when, aged 37, Agricola was appointed governor, *legatus Augusti pro praetore*, of Britannia by Vespasianus (AD 77). The emperor himself had served, with distinction, in the original expedition to the island under Claudius (Suetonius *Divus Vespasianus* 4.1). There was a particular factor in the choice of Agricola as governor of Britannia He was a strong supporter of the Flavian dynasty, having gone over to Vespasianus (March AD 69), as implied by Tacitus (*Agricola* 7.2), before the would-be emperor had even publicly declared his hand (July AD 69). He had also served in the province twice before, as a *tribunus laticlavius* during the Boudican revolt (AD 61) and as the legate of *XX Valeria Victrix* during the conquest of the Brigantes (AD 70–73). Agricola, unusually for a Roman governor, came to the province with considerable local knowledge and experience.

It goes without saying that our knowledge of Agricola's tenure as governor is greatly enhanced by Tacitus' brief biography (or perhaps hagiography) of his father-in-law. Some care, however, should be taken when using the *Agricola* (*de vita Iulii Argicolae*) as a source since it is a laudatory biography written as an act of devotion (*pietas*). But the fact remains that much of what this vital source covers is probably true even if the credit need not be entirely accorded to Agricola.

Agricola sought military glory and from the start he was 'anxious and eager for action' (Tacitus *Agricola* 5.1). His first action was the suppression of the Ordovices of what are now central and north Wales and the reoccupation of Mona, now the island of Anglesey (AD 77). Agricola had arrived in the province late in the year and thus the following summer (AD 78) was his first full campaigning season. It is usually assumed that this season's campaign was in the territory of the Brigantes where, according to Tacitus (ibid. 20.3), he built forts, although some of this period might have been spent north of the Solway in what is now southern Scotland: measures to promote, as Tacitus stresses (ibid. 21), 'Romanization'. As he also operated there during his third season (AD 79), ravaging tribes as far north as the estuary of the Tanaus (Tay). Again, according to Tacitus (ibid. 22.1) he built forts. The following year (AD 80) saw Agricola consolidating on a line between the Clota and Bodotria (Clyde and Forth) with clearly no advances the next year either: Tacitus says (ibid. 23) the isthmus was firmly held by garrisons (*praesidia*), though he did operate in the south-west of Scotland: Tacitus merely says Agricola advanced through 'repeated and successful battles' (ibid. 24.1). There were, however, the campaigns north of the Bodotria against the Caledonii, his sixth (AD 82), when victory narrowly eluded him – *VIIII Hispana* was badly mauled during a night attack upon its marching camp – and his seventh (AD 83), which culminated in Mons Graupius. Recalled in spring AD 84, he was denied further appointments because of, so Tacitus alleges (ibid. 41.4, cf. Cassius Dio 60.20.3), Domitianus' malice and jealousy.

Whether the allegation is justified, Tacitus certainly believed his father-in-law was hated and distrusted by the emperor because he was a good man and a successful commander. As a commander in the field Agricola displayed sound judgement and stout courage, and did not shrink from toil and danger. Brave and decisive under pressure, he led the troops personally and chose camp sites himself (Tacitus *Agricola* 18.4–5, 20.2, 22.1, 35). In other words, Tacitus' father-in-law had all the usual attributes of the good Roman general.

With *V Alaudae*, *XXI Rapax* and *vexillationes* from the five other Rhine legions absent in Italy, the nobleman C. Iulius Civilis, under a cloak of loyalty to Vespasianus, had roused his fellow Batavi against Vitellius. The rebel alliance, besides Civilis' own people, consisted of Germanic tribes who contributed *auxilia* to Rome, and Germanic tribes further east of the Rhine. When Vitellius was overthrown, Civilis should have placed himself at the disposal of Vespasianus. But many of the Gallic auxiliaries in Gallia Belgica, including the Tungri, deserted Rome and four of the Rhine legions swore loyalty to the rebels. Civilis' head was evidently turned. Once the new emperor had regained control of Italy, a powerful expeditionary force under the consul Q. Petilius Cerialis, son-in-law of Vespasianus and a reckless but able commander, was sent to the Rhine. Civilis' forces were decisively crushed in battle at Trever (Trier) in AD 70.

After the rebellion the two-legion camp at Vetera, reconstructed in stone under Nero but heavily damaged during the recent battle there, was replaced by a new fortress for just one legion, *XXII Primigenia pia fidelis*, which had gallantly held the camp at Moguntiacum. At the same time, four other Rhine legions (*I Germanica*, *IIII Macedonia*, *XV Primigenia* and *XVI Gallica*) were disbanded for having seriously disgraced themselves. Of the other two legions, completely uninvolved in the rebellion, *V Alaudae* was posted to Moesia, and *XXI Rapax* was left on the Rhine but moved to the rebuilt camp at Bonna. Mogontiacum now became the home of *I Adiutrix* and *XIIII Gemina Martia Victrix*, the latter unit making a return visit.

It was during the reign of Vespasianus' younger son, Domitianus, that Decebalus rose to prominence, massing a strong force of Dacian warriors, subjecting neighbours, such as the Sarmatians and Bastarnae, and even enlisting deserters from the Roman Army. Cassius Dio describes him in a predictable way, a worthy opponent who was: 'Shrewd in the understanding of warfare and shrewd also in the waging of war; he judged well when to attack and chose the right moment to retreat; he was an expert in ambuscades and master in pitched battle; he knew not only how to follow up a victory well, but also how to manage a defeat' (Cassius Dio 67.6.1).

Under the king's aggressive leadership, the Dacians raided across the Danube and inflicted serious defeats on the Romans. Domitianus' campaign against them ended in what amounted to a fiasco, with a treaty by which the Romans paid Decebalus an annual indemnity and provided him with the services of engineers so that he could upgrade the fastnesses of his kingdom. Therefore it comes as no surprise to find Traianus, when he donned the purple, seeking terms that were favourable to Rome.

In the first campaign the Dacians initially fell back, avoiding a pitched battle, and the Romans consolidated their gains. During the winter Decebalus launched a counterattack somewhere in Moesia Inferior, which was repulsed. Having surveyed the difficult terrain in the approach from the west to Sarmizegetusa, the Dacian capital set high in the Carpathians, Traianus for the second season decided to advance from the east towards the Red Tower Pass.

Trajan's Column is outstanding, not only for its size, but also in the idea of recording in detail the progress of an imperial campaign. Naturally, throughout the story the emperor has a dominant position, not only in artistic portrayal, but also in the frequency of his appearance. It seems Traianus directed every move in his two Dacian wars. (Fields-Carré Collection)

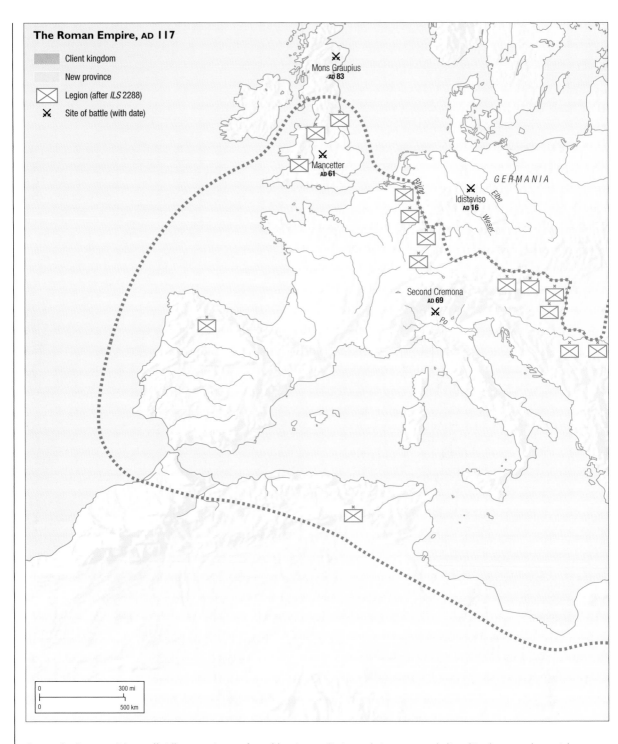

The Roman Empire, AD 117

- Client kingdom
- New province
- ☒ Legion (after *ILS* 2288)
- ✖ Site of battle (with date)

Mons Graupius
AD **83**

Mancetter
AD **61**

GERMANIA

Idistaviso
AD **16**

Second Cremona
AD **69**

Rhine

Elbe

Weser

Po

| 0 | 300 mi |
| 0 | 500 km |

As yet, the Romans did not officially recognize any formal barriers or limits to their power, and client kingdoms on the periphery of Roman territory acted as buffer states as well as providing troops and an easy route to further expansion when required. Despite Augustus' strict instructions to his successor, the impetus for expansion remained and new provinces were added throughout the following century. The southern part of Britannia was annexed (AD 43) and other peripheral areas like Cappadocia (AD 17), Thrace (AD 46), Commagene (AD 72) and Arabia (AD 106) were absorbed. As these client kingdoms were eliminated Roman forces became directly responsible for the defence of a growing proportion of the empire's boundaries.

At other times, however, the irresistible urge for grand conquest and triumphal glory proved too strong, and emperors ventured further afield, even to the outermost edge of the world itself. Thus the acquisition of southern Britannia by Claudius (AD 43), which brought nothing of real value and pulled the Romans further from their Mediterranean focus, or the conquest of Dacia by Traianus

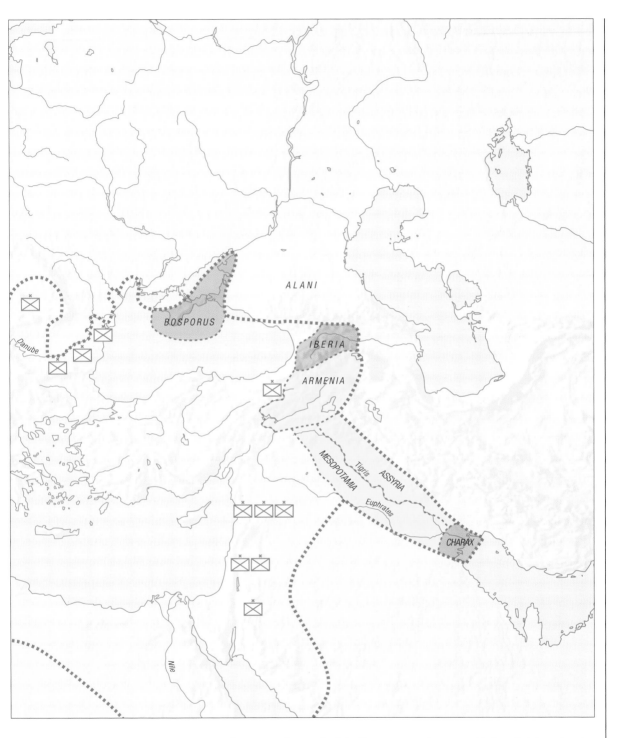

(AD 101–06), which may have removed a long-standing menace but involved the Romans more than ever with the tribal dynamics of central Europe. In the east the age-old rivalry between Rome and Parthia required periodic demonstrations of Roman posture and resolve, involving as ever the kingdom of Armenia to which both superpowers laid claim.

Traianus' great Parthian campaign (AD 114–17) resulted in the formation of three new provinces – Armenia, Mesopotamia and Assyria. The death of Traianus, however, put an end to all further conquest, and his successor Hadrianus withdrew the advanced troops and organized the eastern frontier on the banks of the Euphrates. The best explanation for Traianus' eastern conquests, therefore, seems to be a 'desire for glory', as suggested by Cassius Dio when he says (68.17.2) the Parthians were prepared to negotiate in the usual way about Armenian sovereignty. Certainly the sheer size of the invasion force – some 17 of the 30 legions went in their entirety or as substantial *vexillationes* – points to total conquest rather than the traditional scrap over Armenia.

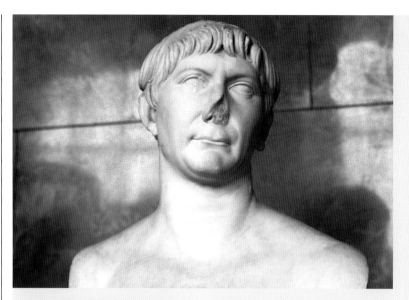

M. Ulpius Traianus (AD 56–117)

Traianus was the first emperor who was not born in Italy. He came from a family that had emigrated from Umbria to Italica, a town in south-eastern Iberia. His father and namesake had had a brilliant career in the army, and the young Traianus would follow in his footsteps. As a *tribunus militum laticlavius*, he served in Syria, under his father's command, and on the Rhine, where he experienced action against the local tribes. The late eighties saw him as the legate of *VII Gemina* (née *Hispana/Galbiana*) peacefully settled in Legio (Léon). Indeed, his career did not stagnate at all during Domitianus' 'reign of terror'; on the contrary, he made it all the way to the consulship, a slice of information not mentioned in the panegyric given to Traianus by Pliny. At the time of his elevation to the purple Traianus was the *legatus Augusti pro praetore* of Germania Superior.

The chief feature of Traianus' administration was his very good relations with the Senate, which allowed him to accomplish whatever he wished without general opposition. Like Augustus, his *auctoritas*, prestige, was more important than his *imperium*, power. At the very beginning of Traianus' reign, Tacitus (*Agricola* 3.1) spoke of the newly won compatibility of one-man rule and individual liberty established by Nerva and expanded by Traianus. Tacitus later comments (ibid. 44.5), when speaking of his father-in-law's death, that Agricola had forecast the principate of Traianus but had died too soon to see it.

Whether one believes that Principate and liberty had truly been made compatible or not, this evidently was the belief of the aristocracy of Rome. Traianus, by character and actions, contributed to this belief, and he undertook to reward his associates with high office and significant promotions. Of course, the contemporary satirist Juvenal, in one of his best-known judgements, bitterly laments that the citizen of Rome, once master of the world, was now content with just 'bread and circuses' (*panem et circenses*, *Satires* 10.81).

Traianus' reputation remained unimpaired, in spite of the ultimate failure of his costly Parthian war. Early in his reign, after successes in Dacia, he had unofficially been honoured with the title Optimus, 'the best', which long described him even before it became, in AD 114, part of his official titulature. His correspondence with Pliny enables posterity to gain an intimate sense of the emperor in action. His concern for justice and the well being of his subjects is underscored by his comment to Pliny, when faced with the question of the Christians, that they were not to be sought out, 'nor is it appropriate to our age' (*Epistles* 10.97.2).

It is in Traianus that we most see the embodiment of the energetic warrior-emperor. According to Pliny, Traianus joined in the military exercises, sharing the heat and thirst of his soldiers and comforting the fatigued and the sick. He even took a keen interest in weapon training himself, rather than leaving it to a professional instructor. 'It was your custom not to enter your tent until you had inspected the quarters of your fellow soldiers (*commilitones*), and

to retire to bed only after every one else.' On campaign he spent long nights in the open, and sharing his soldiers' labours was both 'an applauder of and witness to' their courage. By this behaviour Traianus won the admiration of his soldiers and succeeded in finding that right blend between the role of commander-in-chief and comrade-in-arms (Pliny *Panegyricus* 13.1–4, 15.3–5, 19.3). Of course Pliny's panegyric contains much that derives from a literary topos, and there is gross exaggeration, but the speech would have to be based on the emperor's known opinions and actions, if it were not to appear insulting or ridiculous. Therefore it seems that Traianus did have the ability to wear the two hats, that is to say, *imperator* and *commilito*.

Dio of Prusa (1.28), also speaking in front of Traianus, observed that in the ideal role the soldiers were much like shepherds who, with the emperor, guarded the flock of the empire. Dio was no doubt well briefed on Traianus' interest in his army and his identification with the soldiers in the performance of their duties. Cassius Dio says (68.8.2) that Traianus marched with his army on foot, made military dispositions in person, and took great care to honour fallen soldiers. Of course the emperor's prolonged wars against the Dacians and the Parthians gave him plenty of opportunity to perform the role of the assiduous fellow soldier. Indeed, the emperor was not afraid to risk his own life and in Mesopotamia was nearly struck by a missile while organizing an attack on the walls of Hatra (ibid. 68.31.3).

Yet it is interesting to note that though Cassius Dio praises Traianus for his bravery, his comments on Traianus' conquests imply that an emperor who 'loved war' was dangerous (68.6.3, cf. 7.5). Like a second Alexander, he got as far as the Persian Gulf, where he supposedly thought aloud: 'I would have crossed over to India if I were a younger man.' The restless warrior-emperor was planning a new season when he suffered a stroke and died soon afterwards.

It was customary for the 4th-century Senate to pray that the incoming emperor might be 'more fortunate than Augustus and better than Trajan' (Eutropius 8.5). In medieval Europe Traianus was held up as an example of the just king, while Dante saw him released from hell, pagan though he was, through the prayer of Pope Gregory; not even the divine Augustus managed that.

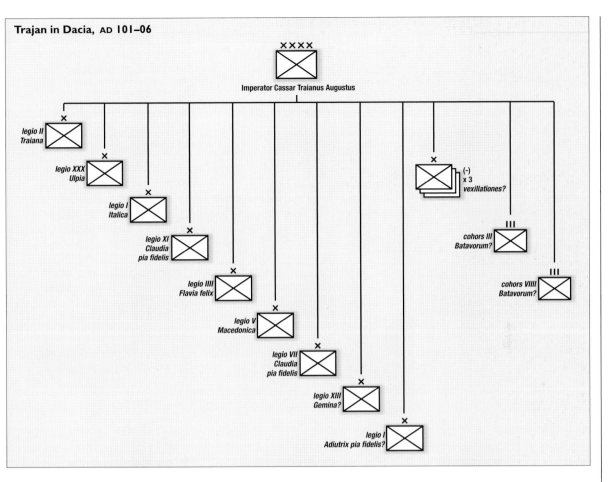

Eventually Sarmizegetusa was reached, but Decebalus capitulated to save his capital from fire and sword, agreeing to the loss of some territory, giving up his engineers, and handing over Roman deserters. Garrisons were left behind while Traianus returned to Rome for his triumph and assumed the title Dacicus. Soon, however, Decebalus felt strong enough to break the peace and the struggle was renewed in AD 105. A grim campaign followed, with much bitter fighting, until Sarmizegetusa fell. The king fled to the north hotly pursed by Roman cavalry, to be brought to bay and driven to take his own life. The head of Decebalus was displayed to the victorious troops. Traianus had the head packed off to Rome and once there it was tossed in the street for the public to gloat over (Trajan's Column scenes cxlv, cxlvii, Cassius Dio 68.14.3).

The Parthian war was the result of a seizure of the throne of Armenia by the Parthian king Osroes for his own nominee. Traianus might have intervened, as was customary, with diplomacy and a show of force, but lured by the vision of Alexander, chose to mount a massive expedition with a view to settling the Parthian problem once and for all. Though there were eight legions already in the east, Traianus called in *XV Apollinaris* from Carnuntum and *vexillationes* from several others. The first moves were into Armenia, but merely to tell the king he no longer occupied the throne. A Roman governor was appointed to the new province, which included Cappadocia.

Traianus, still thirsting for conquests, advanced south into Mesopotamia and occupied Nisibis. He then wintered in Antioch. In the following spring the army was ready for another advance, this time towards Ctesiphon, the Parthian capital. Osroes, troubled by internal dissension, was unable to offer serious resistance and his capital fell after a short siege. It is possible that Traianus,

Traianus assembled on the lower Danube a force of at least nine legions at full strength, with *vexillationes* from other provinces. Raising two new legions, *II Traiana* and *XXX Ulpia*, he also summoned *XI Claudia pia fidelis* from the Rhine frontier. As for the other formations, little is known; in the two wars only five, from the distinctions conferred upon them, can be identified for sure, namely *I Italica, IIII Flavia felix, V Macedonica, VII Claudia pia fidelis*, and probably *XIII Gemina*. The last legion was definitely detailed as part of the garrison of the new province of Dacia, as was *I Adiutrix pia fidelis*. As for *auxilia*, we do know that *cohortes III* and *VIIII Batavorum* were transferred from Britannia to the Danube in AD 104, perhaps as part of the build-up to the second war.

following in the wake of Alexander, marched down to the Persian Gulf and created a client kingdom there, bringing the whole of the great trade route to India and beyond under Roman control. This was the peak of Traianus' achievements, and the high-water mark of the Roman Empire. Yet these conquests so easily won proved more difficult to hold.

Saltus Teutoburgiensis, a province lost

Late in the summer of AD 9 three legions led by P. Quinctilius Varus ventured into Saltus Teutoburgiensis, but they were ambushed and wiped out by Germanic warriors led by Arminius. This ignominious defeat put an end to the Roman expansion east of the Rhine. From then on the ageing Augustus pursued a policy of consolidation. It seems the mistake had been made at Rome by underestimating the force needed to keep Germania pacified and the time necessary for the Germans to become 'Romanized' (Wells 1972: 239).

Arminius, chieftain of the Cherusci, was also C. Iulius Arminius, citizen of Rome, whom Varus believed to be firmly pro-Roman. After all, he had served in the army as a commander in the *auxilia*, which granted him equestrian rank, and on Rome's behalf he had distinguished himself on the field of battle (Velleius Paterculus 2.118.1–2). Anyway, Arminius had informed Varus of the

Tombstone of Marcus Caelius, *primus pilus* of *legio XVIII*, found near Birten-Xanten-Vetera (Bonn, Rheinisches Landesmuseum). The inscription (*ILS* 2244) says he fell, aged 53, in the Varian disaster, so this fine memorial did not mark his mortal remains. He carries a *vitis*, his badge of office, is loaded with *armillae*, torques and *phalerae*, and wears a *corona civica*. (Fields-Carré Collection)

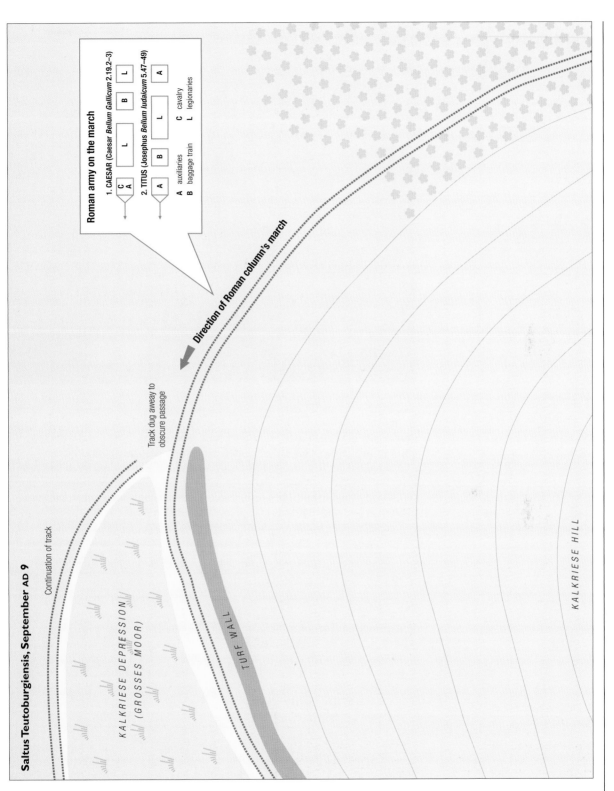

Saltus Teutoburgiensis, September AD 9

Roman army on the march

1. CAESAR (Caesar *Bellum Gallicum* 2.19.2–3)

C / A — L — B — L

2. TITUS (Josephus *Bellum Iudaicum* 5.47–49)

A — B — L — A

A auxiliaries   C cavalry
B baggage train L legionaries

Direction of Roman column's march

Track dug away to obscure passage

Continuation of track

KALKRIESE DEPRESSION
(GROSSES MOOR)

TURF WALL

KALKRIESE HILL

The appointment P. Quinctilius Varus (*cos.* 13 BC) as *legatus Augusti pro praetore* of Germania, with the army on the Rhine under his direct control, may have reflected a policy of bringing the territory under Roman law and organizing it into a province. Varus was an eminent lawyer without any of the obvious military talents of his predecessors; he was also the husband of Augustus' grandniece. Yet it should be noted that previously Varus had successfully served as governor of Syria, quelling the political disturbances in Iudaea following the death of the pro-Roman Herod in 4 BC. Back then his command had consisted of three legions.

possibility of trouble brewing amongst the members of a tribe that lived a couple of days' march west of the summer camp near the Weser. So Varus planned a small detour to his march back to the winter quarters at Vetera, and allowed Arminius to go ahead to rally some of his own tribesmen.

For information about the ambush, we have two very different sources of information. One consists of the accounts written by Roman historians, none of them eyewitnesses to the event, and the other is the archaeological evidence, most of it painstakingly unearthed since the summer of 1987.

Contemporary to the event was Velleius Paterculus, a military man who had served on the Rhine and may have known both Varus and Arminius personally through common service in the army. He places the blame for the disaster on the carelessness of Varus, the treachery of Arminius and the disadvantages of the terrain. His account is abbreviated – he apparently intended to describe the battle in greater detail in another work – but it is colourful despite this:

> An army unexcelled in bravery, the first of Roman armies in discipline, in energy, and in experience in the field, through the negligence of its general, the perfidy of the enemy, and the unkindness of fortune was surrounded. ... Hemmed in by forest and ambuscades, it was exterminated almost to a man by the very enemy whom it has always slaughtered like cattle.
> Velleius Paterculus 2.119.2

The soldier-historian then describes how Varus fell on his sword when all appeared lost, the beheading of Varus' corpse, the delivering of the head to Maroboduus, chief of a tribal confederation on the Danube, and the sending of it on to Augustus in Rome.

Archaeological remains of the battle have been recovered over an area about six by four-and-a-half kilometres in what is known as the Kalkriese–Niewedde Depression, near Osnabrück. Apart from the abundance of Roman coins and military items associated with the Varian disaster, the most exciting find must be the remains of a mile-long sodden wall, with a basal width of about four-and-a-half metres and in places showing evidence of having been topped with a wooden palisade, which the Germanic warriors had obviously constructed well before the Roman column stumbled into the ambuscade.

It is a simple fact that small-scale societies cannot beat sophisticated ones on the open field of battle. But they can defeat them by attacking them in vulnerable situations, especially when they are in a column of march. And so the lightly equipped Germanic warriors, with their superior knowledge of the terrain and greater mobility, defeated the heavily equipped Roman soldiers, with their superior training and better discipline. Such was the Varian disaster.

Mancetter, a province saved

With the bulk of Roman forces on campaign in what is now north Wales, Boudica faced minimal resistance. The provincial towns of Camulodunum (Colchester), Londinium (London) and Verulamium (near St Albans) were quickly overrun and sacked, and a *vexillatio* of *VIIII Hispana*, under the command of Petilius Cerialis, ambushed and destroyed.

Breaking off his Silurian campaign, the governor, Suetonius Paulinus, hastened south-east with a small escort. Deciding to abandon Londinium to its fate, Suetonius Paulinus rejoined his army on its long march down Watling Street (the modern A5). At his disposal were *XIIII Gemina* and a *vexillatio* of *XX Valeria* and those auxiliaries he was able to summon from nearby camps, in all a force of some 10,000 men. The governor had dispatched urgent messages summoning *II Augusta* from its station in the south-west, but for some mysterious reason its acting commander, the *praefectus castrorum* Poenius Postumus, failed to respond.

What Suetonius Paulinus feared above all was a protracted guerrilla war, but elated by her earlier victories Boudica staked all on one battle. According to Tacitus, our chief source for the revolt, Suetonius Paulinus drew up his forces along a defile – legionaries in the centre with auxiliary *cohortes* alongside and *alae* on the wings – with dense woodland protecting his rear. When battle was joined, the legionaries discharged their *pila* into the oncoming Britons. They then pressed forwards, battering at the enemy with their shields and doing murderous work with their swords.

Tacitus makes it seem simple and quickly over, but the account of Cassius Dio (62.12), though garbled, states the battle lasted all day – a more likely story. Anyway, confident of victory, the Britons had brought along their womenfolk to watch the spectacle from wagons positioned behind the war bands. In the Roman advance, however, the Britons soon found themselves crushed against the wagons. Even women and draught animals were slaughtered in the Roman fury that followed. Tacitus says 80,000 of the enemy fell, for the loss of only 400 Romans. Sadly, he gives no clues as to the actual whereabouts of this battle site, although a case has been made for the village of Mancetter near Nuneaton in Warwickshire.

In a single day the back of the rebellion had been broken, and soon after the battle Boudica took her own life. Suetonius Paulinus, now heavily reinforced by units from the Rhine, concentrated his efforts against the Iceni and Trinovantes. Their territory was laid waste by fire and sword, and a chain of forts constructed across eastern Britannia.

Second Cremona, a throne won

This crucial engagement was fought through the night, with victory going to the Flavians as dawn broke: at first light *III Gallica*, a crack Syrian legion, turned to salute the rising sun in their customary way and this created rumours of reinforcements, heartening the dog-tired Flavians and striking dismay into the equally exhausted Vitellians (Tacitus *Historiae* 3.24.3–25.1). The nocturnal phase of the engagement, despite the full moon, had been a confused and

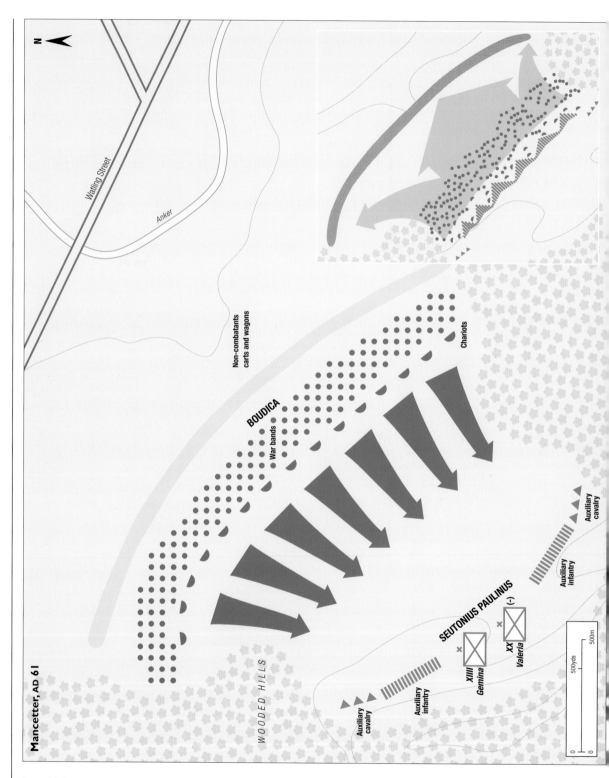

Mancetter, AD 61

Watling Street

Anker

Non-combatants
carts and wagons

BOUDICA

War bands

Chariots

WOODED HILLS

SEUTONIUS PAULINUS

Auxiliary
cavalry

Auxiliary
infantry

XIIII
Gemina

XX
Valeria

(-)

Auxiliary
infantry

Auxiliary
cavalry

500yds

500m

In AD 60 Prasutagus, the client king of the Iceni, died leaving half his possessions to the emperor. He had hoped this would protect his kingdom and family, but the Romans decided otherwise and incorporated his kingdom, which covered large parts of today's East Anglia, into the province. When his queen Boudica protested, she was flogged and her daughters raped (Tacitus *Annales* 14.31.2). Boudica raised the Iceni in revolt, who were quickly joined by their neighbours the Trinovantes, a tribe that inhabited parts of today's Suffolk and Essex. The underlying cause of the revolt was the harsh and oppressive Roman occupation and administration of Britannia: licentious soldiers, voracious tax collectors and 'noble savages' are commonplace themes in Tacitus, but the commonplace is often true.

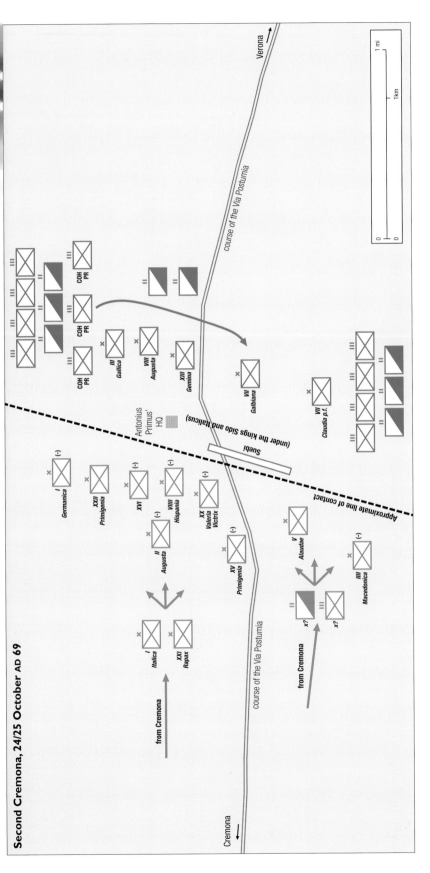

Second Cremona, 24/25 October AD 69

Verona

course of the Via Postumia

1 mi

1km

COH PR

COH PR

COH PR

COH PR

II
Gallica

VIII
Augusta

XIII
Gemina

VII
Galbiana

VII
Claudia p.f.

Antonius
Primus'
HQ

Suebi
(under the kings Sido and Italicus)

Approximate line of contact

I
Germanica

XXII
Primigenia

XVI

VIIII
Hispania

II
Augusta

XX
Valeria
Victrix

XV
Primigenia

V
Alaudae

IIII
Macedonica

I
Italica

XXI
Rapax

from Cremona

course of the Via Postumia

from Cremona

x?

x?

Cremona

The civil war battle of Second Cremona was the critical engagement that decided the outcome of the 'Year of the Four Emperors'. Back in August, Vespasianus had met with his advisors and backers at Berytus (Beirut) and perfected their plan of campaign. C. Licinius Mucianus, governor of Syria, was to march on Italy; Vespasianus, the emperor-to-be, was to starve Rome into submission from Egypt and Africa by cutting off the grain supply; and meanwhile the legions of Pannonia would block the Alps until they and those of Moesia were taken over by Mucianus. As for the Rhine legions, already depleted by the *vexillationes* dispatched to Italy, they would be paralyzsed by a mock revolt staged by the Batavi at the mouth of the Rhine. Almost without a blow, Italy would fall into the lap of Vespasianus. But others were ready to strike hard and strike fast. The Danube legions were eager to supplant those of the Rhine, and they had a natural and gifted leader in the restless Antonius Primus, legate of *legio VII Galbiana*.

Decapitated bronze head from a statue of Claudius (London, British Museum, P&E 1965 12-11), found in the river Alde, Suffolk. It is believed to have been looted from Colchester-Camulodunum during its sack by Boudica, who seemed hell-bent on destroying every trace of Rome. (Ancient Art & Architecture)

bitter affair and, as Tacitus says, 'on both sides weapons and uniforms were the same, frequent challenges and replies disclosed the watchword and standards were inextricably confused as they were captured by this group or that and carried hither and thither' (ibid. 3.22.3).

A civil war creates stronger passions and tends to produce shocking events, and the climax of Second Cremona was to be no exception. The Vitellian camp had been built at no great distance from the walls and suburbs of Cremona on the north-east, between the converging road from Brixia and the Via Postumia, and near their junction. When the main (southern) gate of the camp was finally forced, the surviving Vitellians threw themselves down from the ramparts and took shelter in nearby Cremona. Despite a show of surrender, the inhabitants of this affluent town fell victim to indiscriminate rape and slaughter. A signal atrocity had occurred in this final phase – the killing of a father by his son (ibid. 3.25.2) – and the sack of a Roman provincial town by Roman soldiers would send a thrill of horror through the empire.

Mons Graupius, a battle too far

Assembled under the leadership of Calgacus ('the Swordsman', cf. Middle Irish *colg* 'sword'), 'the full force of all' the Caledonian tribes, 30,000 warriors, occupied the slopes of Mons Graupius (Tacitus *Agricola* 29.3–4). The size of Agricola's army is not given, but Tacitus does say the enemy had a 'great superiority in numbers' (ibid. 35.4). Agricola certainly had 8,000 auxiliary infantry and probably 5,000 auxiliary cavalry together with *vexillationes* from the four legions (*II Adiutrix pia fidelis*, *II Augusta*, *VIIII Hispana* and *XX Valeria Victrix*) of Britannia (ibid. 35.2, 37.1), giving perhaps a total force of some 20,000 (St Joseph 1978: 283).

Tacitus does name some of the auxiliary units present on the day: four *cohortes* of Batavi, two *cohortes* of Tungri (ibid. 36.1), and an unspecified number of Britons recruited from the tribes in the south long since conquered (ibid. 29.2). The actual identification of these units is not certain, but we do know that *cohors I Tungrorum* is the earliest attested garrison at Vindolanda (*Tab. Vindol.* II 154), leaving there soon after AD 90 to be replaced by *cohors VIIII Batavorum* (ibid. II 159, 282, 396). The Britons themselves may have been present in their own ethnic cohort, a *cohors Brittonum*, for Tacitus mentions elsewhere (*Historiae* 1.70.3) cohorts of Brittones at First Cremona fighting for the Vitellian cause.

Fearing that he might be outflanked, Agricola deployed the auxiliary *cohortes* in the centre, with their ranks opened out, and 3,000 horsemen on the wings, which probably comprised six *alae quingenariae*. A further four *alae quingenariae*, some 2,000 horsemen, were kept in reserve. The legionary *vexillationes* were to the rear, drawn up in front of the marching camp. The Caledonii were deployed in closed-packed tiers on the gentle slope with their van on the level ground.

The Caledonian war chariots raced across the ground between the two armies, only to be driven off by the Roman *alae*. Next up was a brisk exchange of missiles followed by the Roman advance up the slope. 'Striking them with the bosses of their shields, and stabbing them in the face' (Tacitus *Agricola* 36.2), the auxiliary infantrymen were initially successful and soon joined by the *alae*. The sheer numbers of the Caledonii, however, combined with the roughness of the terrain, halted this advance and gradually the auxiliaries began to be outflanked. In a counter-move Agricola sent in his reserve *alae*, which stemmed the flanking movement and then, in turn, fell on the rear of the war bands, which accordingly broke. The legionaries had not been engaged. This was an achievement that occasioned one of Tacitus' characteristic epigrams: 'a great victory glorious for costing no Roman blood' (ibid. 35.2).

The exact location of the battle of Mons Graupius is unknown. However, below the Iron Age hill fort of Mither Tap o' Bennachie, the most north-easterly mountain in Aberdeenshire and on the border between the Highlands and the Lowlands, has been suggested as a possible site. View looking south-west from Mill of Carden. (Fields-Carré Collection)

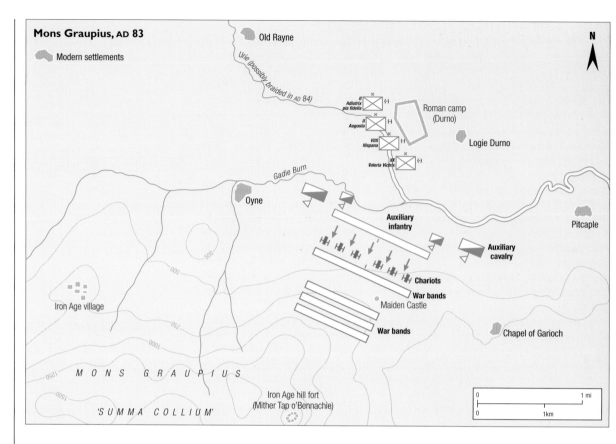

Mons Graupius, AD 83

Modern settlements

N

Old Rayne

Urie (possibly braided in AD 84)

II Adiutrix pia fidelis

II Augusta

VIIII Hispana

XX Valeria Vidrix

Roman camp (Durno)

Logie Durno

Gadie Burn

Oyne

Pitcaple

Auxiliary infantry

Auxiliary cavalry

Chariots

War bands

Maiden Castle

Iron Age village

War bands

Chapel of Garioch

M O N S   G R A U P I U S

Iron Age hill fort (Mither Tap o'Bennachie)

'S U M M A   C O L L I U M'

0   1 mi
0   1km

There have been many attempts to locate the site of the battle, but all we really know is what Tacitus tells us and, sufficient to say, none of his evidence is over-helpful. Nevertheless, the ubiquitous instrument of Roman mobility was the marching camp, and those of Agricola that stretch north and north-west in a great arc from near Stonehaven to the pass of Grange just east of the Spey are useful pointers. Several criteria can be used to identify those marching camps most conceivably the work of Agricolan legions. They include a tendency to squareness of plan, and a method of gateway defence incorporating the *clavicula*, an extended arc of ditch and rampart that compelled an attacker to expose his right or unshielded side to the camp's defenders.

At Logie Durno near Pitcaple, 9.6km (six miles) north-west of Inverurie is a marching camp of some 58.25ha. Unfortunately the camp, the largest known beyond the Forth and big enough to accommodate Agricola's entire force with room to spare, is undated. However, a persuasive case was made out by St Joseph (1978) for identifying it as Agricola's base on the eve of the battle, which (it has been suggested) was fought out on the lower slopes of Bennachie, 4.8km (three miles) to the south-west.

Pax Romana

Imperialism implies a conscious desire to conquer, and if it is to carry weight in the historical balance, it must lead to some spectacular and abiding achievement. The expression *pax Romana*, adopted from the elder Pliny, was used by that polymath incidentally, in describing plants 'now available to the botanist from all the corners of the world, thanks to the boundless majesty of Roman peace' (*Historia Naturalis* 27.1.3). But *pax Romana* should not be sneezed at, especially if we consider the terrible plight of our own world today. Despite notable exceptions, the empire and its armed frontiers were relatively quiet for two centuries. This was something new, as yet to be repeated, to the human condition.

In its broad outline, the manifest destiny of Rome was devastatingly simple. The mood of the time, if correctly reflected in the literature of the day, leans unmistakably toward irresistible expansion beyond the confines of the Italy on the grounds of mission, decreed fortune and divine will. Take, for instance, the elder Pliny on the role of the Italian Peninsula and the Latin language: 'A land chosen by divine providence to unify empires so disparate and races so manifold; to bring to a common concord so rough, discordant voices; to give culture to mankind; to become, in short, the world's homeland' (Pliny *Historia Naturalis* 3.5.39).

An altruistic view to say the least. 'The Gods favour us', says Tacitus (*Germania* 33.1) more tersely, while the Augustan poet Virgil has Iuppiter himself proclaim: 'On them [the Romans] I impose no limits of time or place. I have given them an empire that will know no end' (*Aeneid* 1.278–79 West). In earthly terms *pax Romana* would be an enormous human entity – enormous for the times that is (conventionally estimated at about 55 million souls) – spread over an area that was also enormous (nearly five million square kilometres). The civilized Romans, on whom divine providence had bestowed earth's fairest portion, evidently marched ahead with full belief in their right to world dominion.

Josephus, albeit now a protégé of Vespasianus, does not hesitate to equate Rome's outward march with megalomania:

> And even the world is not big enough to satisfy them; the Euphrates is not far enough to the east, or the Danube to the north, or Libya and the desert beyond to the south, or Gades to the west; but beyond the Ocean they have sought a new world, carrying their arms as far as Britannia, that land of mystery.
> *Bellum Iudaicum* 2.363

A Greek quip, once relayed by Cicero, might best describe the credible opinion at the street level: 'No matter that they hate us, as long as they fear us' (*Philippics* 1.14). Of course, as is customary with all polyglot empires, there is also a reactionary backlash to Rome's cosmopolitanism and cultural flexibility that readily finds its street-tongue through overt racism:

> Upon my word, I was wanting to give him [Claudius] a fraction of time more, until he had endowed with citizenship those tiny few who are left over (for he had resolved to see all Greeks, Gauls, Iberians and Britons wearing the toga). But since it is your pleasure that some foreigners should be left for propagation, and since you command it to be so, so be it.
> Clotho, one of the Three Fates, to Mercury, in Seneca *Apocolocyntosis* 3.3

Portrait statue of Claudius as Iuppiter, from Lanuvium (Vatican City, Musei Vaticani). In his capacity of censor, this far-sighted emperor not only allowed prominent Gauls into the Senate but also pushed through a resolution to grant civil rights to the provinces as a whole. Taking its cue from the Prima Porta Augustus, this portrayal of Claudius depicts him as a benign cosmocrat. (akg-images)

The wearing of the toga was a distinctive right, under Augustus a duty (Suetonius *Divus Augustus* 40.5), of the Roman citizen (Virgil *Aeneid* 1.282). Of course this is blatant exaggeration, for out of the world population in AD 48 Claudius himself as censor registered only 5,984,072 Roman citizens (Tacitus *Annales* 11.25.8). Also, as censor, Claudius gave 'trousered, long-haired Gauls', who were citizens, the right to hold office in Rome and introduced a number of them into the Senate (Lyons Tablet, *CIL* 13.1668 col. 2, cf. Tacitus *Annales* 1.23–25). Although this farsighted policy led to integration and stability, Seneca obviously mocks him for this.

We can credit the progressive but eccentric Claudius with a concept of the unity of the empire, an empire in which the conquered, whatever their race, profited as much as the conquerors from *pax Romana*. However, bigotry and understanding are strange bedfellows at the best of times, and within the empire, despite the wisdom of emperors such as Claudius in taking the longer view, there was a permanent division between the conquered and their conquerors. Racial intolerance is an insidious thread that runs throughout human history. In this the British Empire was no better (or worse) than that of Rome. Take, for instance, the forthright views of Cecil John Rhodes

(1853–1902), the British imperialist and industrialist who founded Rhodesia (Zimbabwe) with the help of the Maxim machine gun:

> Whites have clearly come out top ... in the struggle for existence. ... Within the white race the English-speaking man has proved himself to be the most likely instrument of the Divine plan to spread Justice, Liberty, and Peace over the widest possible area of the planet. Therefore I shall devote the rest of my life to God's purpose and help him to make the world English.
>
> C. J. Rhodes, November 1893

Later, as the Prime Minister and virtual dictator of the Cape Colony, the 'Colonial Colossus' would speak of British dominion of the African continent 'from the Cape to Cairo'. Empires naturally create a culture of pride and pomp, and foster the rhetoric of racial superiority. The imperial poets Virgil and Kipling both supplied their readers with panegyrics expounding the grandeur of imperial domain: Romans wanted the prestige of *pax Romana*; and Britons could proudly boast that the sun never set on British shores.

For the British, with their nautical imagination, the Middle Sea was not merely a segmented lake contained by three continents but the corridor to the British Empire, a watery highway from Gibraltar to Goa. Similarly the Romans saw the *Mare nostrum* as an organizing principle, albeit as landlubbers it was buckled firmly at the narrow passage of the Pillars of Hercules against outside intrusion. Naturally the Romans themeselves did not just settle for the sun, the vine and the olive, the province of Britannia is testament alone to that fact.[1] Yet the warm pulse of this expanse of blue water and the fringe of provinces around its shores meant Mediterranean culture circulated well beyond its outer margins.

Of course dreams of boundless empire are but dreams, the divine gift of celestial gods and court poets. In truth world dominion rested on Rome's military arm, whose strength and length were not indefinite. Moreover, with its laws against the bearing of arms, *pax Romana* would eventually create a state whose citizens would forget how to fight. This exemplifies the security problem of the empire and would eventually undermine Rome's self-appointed role as the 'world's policeman'. On the one hand, a cultural gap and disparity of wealth between Rome (the 'First World') and *barbaricum* (the 'Third World') far too big to promise indefinite peace; on the other, advantages in military technology far too small to guarantee a permanent Roman advantage. Time confirms this pessimism. In fact on the field of battle Rome had no secret weapon. It prevailed not through technical superiority but by the fruit of iron discipline, dogged pertinacity, exceptional organization and sanguine reputation. The Roman Army was always at its best in set-piece, face-to-face encounters.

---

1 Cf. Kipling's line: 'Dominion over palm and pine' ('Recessional' 1897).

Chronology

27 BC	Octavianus takes title Augustus, 'the revered one'
26–25 BC	Augustus campaigns in north-west Iberia
22–19 BC	Augustus in the east
20 BC	Crassus' eagles recovered from Parthians
17 BC	Lollian disaster
16–13 BC	Augustus in Gaul, Agrippa in the east
15 BC	Drusus and Tiberius campaign north of the Alps – new provinces of Raetia and Noricum
12–9 BC	Drusus campaigns beyond the Rhine
9 BC	Death of Drusus
9–7 BC	Tiberius campaigns in Germania
6–4 BC	P. Quinctilius Varus governor of Syria
AD 4	Tiberius returns to Germania
AD 6	Pannonian revolt
AD 7	Varus governor of Germania
AD 9	Varian disaster at Saltus Teutoburgiensis
AD 10–11	Tiberius and Germanicus secure Rhine frontier
AD 14	Death of Augustus – northern legions mutiny
AD 15–16	Germanicus campaigns against Arminius of the Cherusci
AD 17	Triumph of Germanicus
AD 17–24	Uprising of Tacfarinas in Numidia
AD 19	Deaths of Germanicus and Arminius
AD 21	Rebellion of Florus and Sacrovir in Gallia Belgica
AD 26	Thracian revolt
AD 26–36	Pontius Pilate procurator of Iudaea
AD 28	Frisian revolt
AD 35–39	Vitellius governor of Syria
AD 37	Birth of Joseph ben Matthias (Josephus)
AD 40–44	Mauretanian revolt – suppressed by C. Suetonius Paulinus
AD 42	Rebellion of Furius Camillus Scribonius, governor of Dalmatia
AD 43	Claudius conquers southern part of Britannia – Vespasianus legate of *II Augusta*
AD 44	Triumph of Claudius
AD 47	Cn. Domitius Corbulo, governor of Germania Inferior, suppresses Frisii
AD 48	P. Ostorius Scapula, governor of Britannia, suppresses Iceni
AD 51	Ostorius Scapula defeats Caratacus – Silures continue to resist
AD 57–63	War with Parthia over Armenia – Domitius Corbulo takes Artaxata and Tigranocerta
AD 60	Suetonius Paulinus, governor of Britannia, captures Mona (Anglesey)
AD 60–61	Uprising of Iceni under Boudica – suppressed by Suetonius Paulinus
AD 64	Fire of Rome
AD 66	Riots in Alexandria
AD 66–74	Jewish revolt
AD 67	Vespasianus subdues Galilee – Josephus surrenders
AD 68	Rebellion of C. Iulius Vindex, governor of Gallia Lugdunensis
AD 68–69	Civil war – 'Year of the Four Emperors'
AD 69	Battles of First and Second Cremona
AD 69–70	Rebellion of C. Iulius Civilis – suppressed by Q. Petilius Cerialis
AD 70	Titus sacks Jerusalem

AD 71	Joint triumph of Vespasianus and Titus
AD 71–73	Petilius Cerialis, governor of Britannia, defeats Brigantes
AD 73–74	L. Flavius Silva, governor of Iudaea, besieges Masada
AD 73–77	Sex. Iulius Frontinus, governor of Britannia, defeats Silures
AD 83	Cn. Iulius Agricola, governor of Britannia, defeats Caledonii at Mons Graupius
AD 85–89	War with Decebalus of Dacia
AD 86	Chatti cross Rhine
AD 89	Rebellion of L. Antonius Saturninus, governor of Germania Superior
AD 101–02	Traianus' first Dacian war
AD 105–06	Traianus' second Dacian war – Decebalus commits suicide
AD 114	Rome annexes Armenia
AD 114–17	Traianus' Parthian war
AD 115–17	Uprising of Jewish communities in Egypt, Cyrene and Cyprus

Roman emperors

Iulio-Claudians

27 BC–AD 14	Augustus (Imperator Caesar Augustus)
AD 14–37	Tiberius (Ti. Caesar Augustus)
AD 37–41	Caligula (C. Caesar Augustus Germanicus)
AD 41–54	Claudius (Ti. Claudius Caesar Augustus Germanicus)
AD 54–68	Nero (Imperator Nero Claudius Caesar Augustus Germanicus)

'Year of the Four Emperors'

AD 68–69	Galba (Ser. Sulpicius Galba Imperator Caesar Augustus)
AD 69	Otho (Imperator M. Otho Caesar Augustus)
AD 69	Vitellius (A. Vitellius Augustus Germanicus Imperator)

Flavians

AD 69–79	Vespasianus (Imperator Caesar Vespasianus Augustus)
AD 79–81	Titus (Imperator T. Caesar Vespasianus Augustus)
AD 81–96	Domitianus (Imperator Caesar Domitianus Augustus)

Adoptive Emperors

AD 96–98	Nerva (Imperator Nerva Caesar Augustus)
AD 98–117	Traianus (Imperator Caesar Traianus Augustus)
AD 117–38	Hadrianus (Imperator Caesar Traianus Hadrianus Augustus)

Ancient authors

Only the most frequently cited ancient authors are listed here. Further details about them, and information about other sources, is most conveniently available in *The Oxford Classical Dictionary* (3rd edition). In the following notes Penguin denotes Penguin Classics, and Loeb denotes Loeb Classical Library. The Loeb editions, which are published by Harvard University Press, display an English translation of a text next to the original language. As Virginia Woolf rightly said, 'the Loeb Library, with its Greek or Latin on one side of the page and its English on the other, came as a gift of freedom ... the existence of the amateur was recognised by the publication of this Library'. For the complete index of Loeb editions you should log on to www.hup.harvard.edu/loeb.

Josephus (b. AD 37)

Josephus (T. Flavius Iosephus) was a pro-Roman historian but also a member of the priestly aristocracy of the Jews with a largely rabbinic education. Put in charge of Galilee by the Jerusalem leaders during the Jewish revolt of AD 66–70, he was eventually besieged at Jotapata and taken hostage. Given Roman citizenship and land in Iudaea, Josephus spent most of his life in or around Rome as an advisor and historian to the Flavian emperors, Vespasianus, Titus and Domitianus.

For centuries, the works of Josephus were more widely read in Europe than any book other than the Bible, especially the *Jewish Antiquities* (*Antiquitates Iudaicae*), a history of the Jewish people all the way from Adam down to the eve of the revolt. For us, however, his *Jewish War* (*Bellum Iudaicum*), originally written in Aramaic but later appearing in an amplified Greek translation (Greek had not only been the lingua franca of the east for over three centuries but was also a language accessible to educated Romans), is an invaluable account based on eyewitness testimony and probably the campaign diaries (*commentarii*) of Vespasianus and Titus. Josephus certainly considered that they were valuable sources for the war and, more to the point, failure to use them could have been held against him. His flattery of father and son, especially the latter whom he often simply addresses as Caesar, is both frequent and obvious. The *Bellum Iudaicum* is available in a Penguin edition entitled *The Jewish War*.

Suetonius (b. c. AD 70)

A Latin biographer, Suetonius (C. Suetonius Tranquillus) was a son of the equestrian Suetonius Laetus, a military tribune of *XIII Gemina* who fought on the Othonian side at First Cremona in AD 69. From the correspondence of the younger Pliny he appears to have attracted attention in Rome as an author and scholar by about AD 97, and also gained experience in advocacy. Perhaps intending to pursue the equestrian career, he secured through Pliny's patronage a military tribunate in Britannia sometime around AD 102, which in the event he declined to hold. Subsequently, when Pliny was governor of Bithynia-Pontus in AD 110–12, we find him serving on his staff. It was under the emperors Traianus and Hadrianus that Suetonius held three important posts in the imperial administration, as a fragmentary inscription (*AE* 1953.73) found at his home town of Hippo Regius (Annaba, Algeria), records. As a courtier, for instance, he was likely to have accompanied Hadrianus to the three Gauls, Germania Superior and Inferior, and Britannia in AD 121–22. However, for unknown reasons he was then dismissed from office when the emperor simultaneously deposed as praetorian prefect C. Septicius Clarus, the gentleman Suetonius' collection of 12 imperial biographies (*De vita Caesarum*) was dedicated to.

A striking feature of the biographies is their thematic, rather than the strictly chronological arrangement which his fellow-biographer Plutarch tended to favour. In dealing with the lives of the first emperors, Suetonius does not claim to write history, and there is no evidence of a broad grasp of major issues in his works. He shows, unlike his contemporary Tacitus, little interest in great public or political matters, unless they reflect on the behaviour of his subject. Suetonius, as did Tacitus, wrote a lot about scandalous events and the immoral and pleasure-seeking lifestyles of the Italian aristocrats of the time. Yet he did try to report events fairly and did not attempt to paint every emperor as a power-hungry tyrant who ruled at the expense of traditional Roman rights and freedoms. He thus judges his subjects against a set of popular expectations of imperial behaviour that had taken shape by the time his biographies were composed. Thus Tiberius, Tacitus' *bête noir*, is repeatedly criticized for having failed to live up to expectation, whereas even Nero and Domitianus, rulers on whom Suetonius' final judgement is damning, can nevertheless be commended for having successfully met some of their imperial responsibilities. Suetonius' work is available in both Penguin and Loeb editions.

Tacitus (b. c. AD 56)

Born to an equestrian family in Gallia Narbonensis, perhaps at Vasio, Tacitus (P. or C. Cornelius Tacitus) passed the early years of his life in (for us) complete obscurity. Not even his praenomen is known with certainty. His father was perhaps the equestrian procurator of Gallia Belgica mentioned by the elder Pliny (*Historia Naturalis* 7.76) who served as an officer on the Rhine from around AD 46 to AD 58. Studying oratory at Rome in AD 75, Tacitus was granted the *latus clavus*, that is, the right to wear the broad purple stripe of senatorial rank, by Vespasianus. Shortly thereafter, in AD 77, he married the daughter of Cn. Iulius Agricola, a native from Forum Iulii (Fréjus), a colony and naval station on the coast of Gallia Narbonensis, perhaps while serving his initial military service as *tribunus laticlavius*.

Evidently Tacitus passed quickly through the posts of the junior magistrates of a senatorial career, because he is next attested as praetor in AD 88 (at an early age for a *novus homo*). In the same year he served on the priestly board of the *XV viri sacris faciundis* with Domitianus, who used his position in the college to organize and celebrate the Secular Games. He was abroad (probably as a provincial governor) when his father-in-law Agricola died on 23 August AD 93. On returning to Rome after an absence of three years or more, he was the *consul suffectus* in the second half of AD 97. As consul he delivered the funeral oration for L. Verginius Rufus (Pliny *Epistles* 2.1.6), an honour befitting his reputation as leading orator of the day (ibid. 7.20). In AD 100 he, along with his good friend the younger Pliny, successfully prosecuted Marius Priscus, the former governor of Africa (ibid. 2.11.3).

Thereafter our information on his activities is meagre. We surmise from Pliny (ibid. 6.16.1) that Tacitus was at work on the *Historiae* in circa AD 106, and the chance discovery of an inscription in Asia Minor informs us that Tacitus reached the summit of a senatorial career, *proconsulare* of Asia, in AD 112/13. A passage in the *Annales* (2.61.2) alluding to the extension of Roman dominion to the Red Sea, territory first conquered during Traianus' Parthian campaign of AD 115/16, provides a definite terminus post quem for his death. The succession of Tiberius, which opens the *Annales*, seems to elude the succession of Hadrianus in AD 117, although this is a point of contention. Whether he lived to complete his greatest work we do not know.

With the *Historiae* the reader is repeatedly puzzled or irritated by the absence of information on chronology, topography, strategy and logistics. But Tacitus did not write according to the canons of modern historiography. His aim is to

Formed in 1972, the Ermine Street Guard is, in every sense of the meaning, the mother of all Roman experimental history groups. Best known for their portrayal of *legio XX Valeria Victrix*, the members of the Guard have contributed enormously to our knowledge of Roman military equipment. Here the Guard are putting on an educational display for the general public. (Ancient Art & Architecture)

provide a narrative that will hold the reader's attention, and so his vivid style often reveals his own strong opinions and prejudices.

The subject matter of the *Annales*, for instance, emphasizes Tacitus' hatred for the great concentration of power in the hands of the Iulio-Claudian emperors. However, though he hated the Principate and in his writings tries to paint every emperor as a corrupt despot, he hated civil war and anarchy even more. He had a particularly heavy bias against Tiberius, whom he portrayed as a sinister and cruel emperor, purging his opponents from the Senate by having them tried for treason and executed. He showed scorn for Claudius and Nero, and even his writings about Augustus contained some belittling innuendoes and snide remarks. His writing is full of tales of corruption, government scandal, and innocent people being destroyed or having their good names ruined because of the emperor's lust for power. It was Tacitus' firm belief that the emperor had so much power in his hands that no man could occupy the throne without being corrupted by that power. As Lord Acton would later have it: 'Power corrupts, absolute power corrupts absolutely.' Tacitus' works are available in both Penguin and Loeb editions.

Bibliography

Barker, P., 1981 (4th ed.), *Armies and Enemies of Imperial Rome*, Worthing: Wargames Research Group

Bishop, M. C. & Coulston, J. C. N., 1993, *Roman Military Equipment from the Punic Wars to the Fall of Rome*, London: Batsford

Le Bohec, Y., 1994 (trans. R. Bate 2000), *The Imperial Roman Army*, London: Routledge

Bowman, A. K., 1994 (repr. 2003), *Life and Letters on the Roman Frontier: Vindolanda and its People*, London: British Museum Press

Breeze, D. J., 1969, 'The organization of the legion: the First cohort and the equites legionis', *Journal of Roman Studies* 59: 50–55

Campbell, D. B., 2003, *Greek and Roman Siege Machinery, 399 BC–AD 363*, Oxford: Osprey (New Vanguard 78)

Campbell, J. B., 1984 (repr. 1996), *The Emperor and the Roman Army, 31 BC–AD 235*, Oxford: Clarendon Press

Connolly, P., 1991, 'The Roman fighting technique deduced from armour and weaponry', in V. A. Maxfield & M. J. Dobson (eds.), *Roman Frontier Studies 1989 (Proceedings of the Fifteenth International Congress of Roman Frontier Studies)*, Exeter: Exeter University Press, 358–363

Connolly, P., 1997, '*Pilum, gladius* and *pugio* in the late Republic', *Journal of Roman Military Equipment Studies* 8: 41–57

Davies, R. W., 1989, *Service in the Roman Army*, Edinburgh: Edinburgh University Press

Dobson, B., 1972, 'Legionary centurion or equestrian officer? A comparison of pay and prospects', *Ancient Society* 3: 193–207

Du Picq, Charles-Ardant, 1903 (trans. Col. J. Greely & Maj. R. Cotton 1920, repr. 1946), *Battle Studies: Ancient and Modern*, Harrisburg: US Army War College

Feugère, M., 1993 (trans. D. G. Smith 2002), *Weapons of the Romans*, Stroud: Tempus

Fields, N., 2004, *Rome's Northern Frontier, AD 70–235*, Oxford: Osprey (Fortress 31)

Fields, N., 2006, *Roman Auxiliary Cavalryman, AD 14–193*, Oxford: Osprey (Warrior 101)

Fields, N., 2008, *The Roman Army: the Civil Wars, 88–31 BC*, Oxford: Osprey (Battle Orders 34)

Franzius, G., 1995, 'Die römischen Funde aus Kalkriese 1987–95', *Journal of Roman Military Equipment Studies* 6: 69–88

Goldsworthy, A. K., 1996 (repr. 1998), *The Roman Army at War, 100 BC–AD 200*, Oxford: Clarendon Press

Goldsworthy, A. K., 2000, *Roman Warfare*, London: Cassell

Goldsworthy, A. K., 2003, *The Complete Roman Army*, London: Thames & Hudson

Goldsworthy, A. K., 2003 (repr. 2004), *In the Name of Rome: The Men who Won the Roman Empire*, London: Phoenix

Hanson, W. S., 1991, *Agricola and the Conquest of the North*, London: Batsford

Junkelmann, M., 1991, *Die Legionen des Augustus: Der romische Soldat im archaologischen Experiment*, Mainz-am-Rhein: Philipp von Zabern

Keppie, L. J. F., 1980, 'Mons Graupius: the search for a battlefield', *Scottish Archaeological Forum* 12: 79–88

Keppie, L. J. F, 1984 (repr. 1998), *The Making of the Roman Army: From Republic to Empire*, London: Routledge

Maxwell, G. S., 1989, *A Battle Lost: Romans and Caledonians at Mons Graupius*, Edinburgh: Edinburgh University Press

McLeod, W., 1965, 'The range of the ancient bow', *Phoenix* 19: 1–14

Millar, F. G. B., 1977 (repr. 1992), *The Emperor in the Roman World*, London: Duckworth

Milner, N. P., 1996 (2nd ed.), *Vegetius: Epitome of Military Science*, Liverpool: Liverpool University Press

Parker, H. M. D., 1928 (repr. 1958), *The Roman Legions*, Cambridge: Heffer & Sons

Peterson, D., 1992 (repr. 2003), *The Roman Legions Recreated in Colour Photographs*, Marlborough: Crowood Press

Rainbird, J. S., 1969, 'Tactics at Mons Graupius', *Classical Review* 19: 11–12

Rees, R. D., 2001, 'To be and not to be: Pliny's paradoxical Trajan', *Bulletin of the Institute of Classical Studies* 45: 149–68

Sealey, P. R., 1997, *The Boudican Revolt against Rome*, Princes Risborough: Shire

Smith, R. E., 1958, *Service in the Post-Marian Army*, Manchester: Manchester University Press

Speidel, M. A., 1992, 'Roman army pay scales', *Journal of Roman Studies* 82: 87–106

St Joseph, J. K. S., 1978, 'The camp at Durno, Aberdeenshire and the site of Mons Graupius', *Britannia* 9: 271–87

Syme, R, 1934, 'Some notes on the legions under Augustus', *Journal of Roman Studies* 23: 14–33

Ulbert, G., 1969, '*Gladii* aus Pompeji. Vorarbeiten zu einem Corpus römischer *Gladii*', *Germania* 47: 97–128

Watson, G. R., 1969 (repr. 1983, 1985), *The Roman Soldier*, London: Thames & Hudson

Webster, G., 1979 (2nd ed.), *The Roman Imperial Army*, London: A & C Black

Webster, G., 1993, *Boudicca: The British Revolt against Rome AD 60*, London: Batsford

Wells, C. M., 1972, *The German Policy of Augustus*, Oxford: Clarendon Press

Wells, C. M., 1992 (2nd ed.), *The Roman Empire*, London: Fontana

Wells, P. S., 2003, *The Battle that Stopped Rome*, New York: Norton

Glossary

Aerarium militare	military treasury
Agger	rampart or mound
Ala/alae	cavalry 'wing'
Aquila	'eagle' – standard of *legio* (q.v.)
Aquilifer/aquiliferi	'eagle-bearer' – standard-bearer who carried *aquila* (q.v.)
Armilla/armillae	armband – military decoration
As/asses	copper coin, originally worth 1/10th of *denarius* (q.v.), but retariffed at 16 to the *denarius* at the time of Gracchi
Aureus	gold coin worth 25 *denarii* (q.v.)
Auxilia	auxiliary units or auxiliaries
Ballista/ballistae	stone-throwing torsion-spring catapult
Bucina/bucinae	crooked trumpet or horn used to regulate watches
Bucinator/bucinatores	musician who blew *bucina* (q.v.)
Caliga/caligae	military boot
Centuria/centuriae	basic sub-unit of *cohors* (q.v.)
Centurio/centuriones	officer in command of *centuria* (q.v.)
Cingulum/cinguli	sword belt
Clavicula/claviculae	'little key' – curved extension of rampart protecting gateway
Clipeus/clipi	shield used by *auxilia* (q.v.)
Cohors/cohortes	basic tactical unit of *legio* (q.v.)
Contubernium	'tentful' – mess-unit of eight infantry, ten per *centuria* (q.v.)
Cornicen/cornicines	musician who blew the *cornu*, a horn associated with the standards
Cornicularius	junior officer responsible for clerks in *principia* (q.v.)
Corona/coranae	crown – military decoration generally for *centuriones* (q.v.) and above
	corona absidionalis: crown of grass – awarded for rescuing besieged army
	corona aurea: gold crown – awarded for various exploits
	corona civica: crown of oak leaves – awarded for saving life of a citizen
	corona muralis: mural crown in gold – awarded to first man over enemy's walls
	corona vallaris: rampart crown in gold – awarded to first man over enemy's rampart
Decurio/decuriones	officer in command of *turma* (q.v.)
Denarius/denarii	'ten as piece' – silver coin, now worth 16 *asses* (q.v.)
Dilectus	'choosing' – levying of troops
Duplicarius	second-in-command of *turma* (q.v.)
Equites legionis	mounted legionaries
Focale/focalis	woollen scarf
Fossa/fossae	ditch
Gladius/gladii	cut-and-thrust sword carried by legionaries
Imaginifer/imaginiferi	bearer of *imago imperatoris* (q.v.)
Imago imperatoris	standard bearing image of emperor
Imperium	power, command
Intervallum	open space between rear of rampart and tent lines
Lancea/lancae	light spear
Legatus/legati	'deputy' – subordinate commander
Legio/legiones	principal unit of Roman army
Librarius/librarii	clerk
	librarius horreorum: kept granary records
	librarius depositorum: collected soldiers' savings
	librarius caducorum: secured belongings of those killed in action

Lorica/loricae	body armour
Miles/militis	soldier
Mille passus	'one thousand paces' – Roman mile (1.48km)
Optio/optiones	second-in-command of *centuria* (q.v.)
Origo/origines	origin
Origo castris	'born in the camp' – illegitimate sons born to soldiers
Papilio/papilones	'butterfly' – tent
Pereginus/peregini	non-Roman citizen
Pes/pedis	Roman foot (29.59cm)
Phalera/phalerae	'disc' – military decoration
Pilum/pila	principle throwing weapon of legionaries
Pilum muralis	wooden stake for marching camp defences
Porta decumana	rear gateway of camp
Praefectus castrorum	*legio* (q.v.) third-in-command responsible for logistics
Praefectus cohortis	commander of auxiliary cohort
Praetorium	originally headquarters but now commander's tent or quarters
Principia	headquarters
Proconsul	consul whose command was prolonged
Proletarius/proletarii	Roman citizen of lowest order
Propraetor	praetor whose command was prolonged
Scutum/scuta	shield carried by legionaries
Sesterce/sestertii	brass coin worth 1/4th of *denarius* (q.v.)
Signifer/signiferi	bearer of a standard of *centuria* or *turma* (q.v.)
Signum/signa	standard of *centuria* (q.v.)
Socii	Latin and Italian allies of Rome
Spatha/spathae	cavalry sword
Tabularium/tabularii	record-office
Tesserarius/tesserarii	Junior officer responsible for sentries and work parties in *centuria* (q.v.)
Testudo	'tortoise' – mobile formation entirely protected by roof and walls of overlapping and interlocking *scuta* (q.v.)
Tres militiae	military career-structure of equestrian order
Tribunus/tribunitribune	
Triplex acies	'triple line-of-battle' – threefold battle line of Roman army
Tuba/tubae	trumpet used to signal commander's orders
Tubicen/tubicenes	musician who blew *tuba* (q.v.)
Turma/turmae	basic sub-unit of *ala* (q.v.)
Umbo/umbonis	shield boss
Via praetoria	road leading from *praetorium* (q.v.) of camp to *porta praetoria*
Via principalis	principle road extending across width of camp, from *porta principalis dextra* to *porta principalis sinistra*
Vexillarii	corps of veterans
Vexillatio/vexillationes	detachment
Vexillum	standard of *vexillatio* (q.v.)
Vigiles	watchmen
Vitis	centurion's twisted-vine stick

Legionary titles

Numbers identified legions, like modern army units. However, they were not numbered sequentially or exclusively, such inconsistencies dating from the Republic when new legions were created as occasion demanded, and this tended to persist into the Principate. The consequence is that some legions have the same number. Yet legions had titles, which helped to distinguish them, that reflected their origins. The title itself may reflect one of the following: a nickname; a god; a geographical area; a success; or an origin.

Adiutrix	'Supportive'
Alaudae	'Larks'
Antiqua	'Ancient'
Apollinaris	'Sacred to Apollo' – this god was considered by Augustus to be his protecting deity
Augusta	'Augustan' – reconstituted by Augustus
Claudia	'Claudian' – loyal to Claudius
concors	'United'
Cyrenaica	from service in province of that name
Deiotariana	'Deiotarian' – belonging to Deiotarus, tetrarch of Galatia
Equestris	'Knightly'
felix	'Lucky one'
Ferrata	'Ironclad'
fidelis constans	'True and constant'
firma	'Steadfast'
fortis	'Courageous'
Fretensis	after naval victory over Sex. Pompeius in Fretum Siculum (straits of Messina)
Fulminata	'Thunderbolt-carrier'
Gallica	'Gallic' – served in Gaul
Gemina	'Twin' – one legion made out of two
Germanica	'Germanic' – served on the Rhine
Hispana	'Iberian' – served in Iberia
Hispaniensis	'Stationed in Iberia'
Italica	recruited from Italians
Macedonica	'Macedonian' – served in Macedonia
Martia	'Sacred to Mars'
Minervia	'Sacred to Minerva'
pia fidelis	'Loyal and true'
Primigenia	'First born' – of a new breed of legions
Rapax	'Greedy' – in the sense of sweeping all before it
Sabina	'Sabine' – raised in Sabine country
Scythica	'Scythian' – served in Scythia
Traiana	'Traianic' – belonging to M. Ulpius Traianus
Ulpia	'Ulpian' – belonging to M. Ulpius Traianus
Urbana	'Urban'
Victrix	'Victorious'

During the mutiny of the Pannonian legions, the mutineers wanted to merge the three legions into one. 'But jealousy wrecked this suggestion', says Tacitus, 'because everyone wanted it to take his own legion's name' (*Annales* 1.18.2). To illustrate this *esprit de corps*, let us take one example: *legio VI Victrix pia fidelis*. Raised by Octavianus, perhaps in 41–40 BC for it is attested at his siege of Perusia, this was the legion that hailed Galba as emperor in AD 68. The title *Victrix* may refer to an outstanding victory in Iberia (this legion was originally known as *VI Hispaniensis*), where it had been stationed since 30 BC, while *pia fidelis Domitiana* was awarded by Domitianus, the last epithet being dropped after his death when he suffered *damnatio memoriae*. In AD 122 the unit was transferred from Germania Superior to Britannia, being based at Eburacum (York), and was still present there at the end of the 4th century AD according to the document known as the *Notitia Dignitatum*.

Index